AMERICA'S COVENANT

RONALD STOKES

AMERICA'S COVENANT

World Ahead Press is a division of WND Books. The views and opinions expressed in this book are those of the author and do not necessarily reflect the official policy or position or WND Books.

Paperback ISBN: : 978-1-944212-16-2
eBook ISBN: 978-944212-17-9

Printed in the United States of America
16 17 18 19 20 21 LSI 9 8 7 6 5 4 3 2 1

CONTENTS

FOREWORD

Many historians scratch their collective heads in wonderment over the popularity and reverence paid to the Declaration of Independence. They argue that the Declaration was only one of several highly significant events leading to the decision to declare independence and that it did not express any new ideas that were not common throughout the colonies. What makes it so special?

The significance of the Declaration cannot be confined to the Revolutionary War period. It was the most frequently used and most effective resource for abolitionists in the slavery debate. Slavery advocates could not obfuscate the straightforward pronouncement that God had given everyone equal rights, including liberty. As such, it could be considered the primary instigating factor for the Civil War. By contrast, fighting had been conducted for over a year in the Revolutionary War by the time the Declaration was ratified. At the conclusion of the Civil War, the Constitution was amended to agree with the Declaration.

Pauline Maier illustrates historians' perception of the Declaration in her book, *American Scripture.*[1] In the list of mankind's rights, the most common phraseology derived from Locke was "life, liberty, and property." However, the Declaration says, "life, liberty, and the pursuit of happiness." Maier follows the lead of other historians in treating Thomas Jefferson's use of the right to pursue happiness in place of property as insignificant. Yet, if the Declaration had listed the right of property instead of pursuit of happiness, it would have given the right of property potentially co-equal status with the right of liberty. This interpretation would have neutered abolitionists' arguments from the Declaration by referencing the right to own slaves as property.

Maier references George Mason's draft of the Virginia Declaration of Rights as a possible Jeffersonian source.

> That all men are born equally free and independent, and have certain inherent natural rights, of which they cannot, by any compact, deprive or divert their posterity; among which are the enjoyment of life and liberty, with the means of acquiring and possessing property, and pursuing and obtaining happiness and safety.[2]

She implies there is no difference between Jefferson and Mason, "no one held authority over others by right of birth or as a gift of God."[3]

Rather than citing natural rights of unknown origin, Jefferson declared that mankind has been given certain inalienable rights by God. In his *Notes on the State of Virginia*, he indicated that this change was both intentional and profound. "Can the liberties of a nation be thought secure when we have removed their only firm basis, a conviction in the minds of the people that these liberties are the gift of God? That they are not to be violated but by his wrath? Indeed, I tremble for my country when I reflect that God is just, that his justice cannot sleep forever. . . . The Almighty has no attribute which can take side with us in such a contest."[4]

If slaves were born with inherent rights, slave owners had transgressed against slaves by abrogating those rights. If the rights were endowed by God, slave owners had transgressed against the God, who bestowed those rights. Under Mason's philosophy, no one guarantees rights. The Declaration implies that the judge of creation will ultimately dispense justice.

The difference was profound in the motivation of abolitionists. If everyone obtains rights at birth, Northerners would have tended to let slaves recover those rights for themselves. Viewing the right of liberty as coming from God, abolitionists felt they were doing God's work in opposing slavery. The moral aspect changed the character of the debate precluding compromise while energizing abolitionists.

Maier references Willmoore Kendall, Mel Bradford, and Garry Wills "who have written on Lincoln and his 'inventive' interpretation of the Declaration."[5] She implies that farmers talking over the back fence would be incapable of accurately interpreting the Declaration without a PhD in history or, at a minimum, having read her book. She affirms the argument of Jefferson Davis in his farewell address to Congress that the Declaration must be interpreted solely as a historical document. They argue that the truths are inherently not self-evident but easily misinterpreted by the masses.

Historians seem to marvel that Lincoln could be so easily confused as to believe that people could actually take the idea that God has given equal rights to everyone as a fundamental truth.

While the Maier/Davis understanding was the prevailing view of Southerners through the end of the Civil War, it was ridiculed by abolitionists.

> There is your Declaration of Independence, said he, 'a diplomatic dodge;' adopted merely for the purpose of excusing the rebellious Colonies in the eyes of civilized mankind.—There is your Declaration of Independence, no longer the sacred code of the rights of man, but a hypocritical piece of special pleading, drawn up by a batch of artful pettifoggers, who, when speaking of the rights of man, meant but the privileges of a set of aristocratic slaveholders, but styled it 'the rights of man,' in order to throw dust in the eyes of the world, and to inveigle noble-hearted fools into lending them aid and assistance. There are your boasted revolutionary sires, no longer heroes and sages, but accomplished humbuggers and hypocrites, who said one thing and meant another; who passed counterfeit sentiments as genuine, and obtained arms and money and assistance and sympathy on false pretences! There is your great American revolution, no longer the great champion of universal principles, but a mean Yankee trick—a wooden nutmeg—the most impudent imposition ever practiced upon the whole world![6]

The speech by Carl Schurz accurately expresses the full implications of the Maier/Davis interpretation. The Declaration itself states that the views contained therein are self-evident, implying that the obvious understanding of the words is the correct one. Self-evident truths do not depend on existing situations. To the extent that Lincoln misunderstood or misinterpreted the Declaration, he understated its importance.

The final sentence of the Declaration is an oath. "And for the Support of this Declaration, with a firm reliance on the protection of Divine Providence, we mutually pledge to each other our lives, our fortunes, and our sacred honor." What was required for compliance? Who would ensure pledged items were forfeited? Were children and descendants included in this pledge? Would future immigrants be included? Historical events provide answers to these questions. The implications are ominous indeed, and few today are even aware what the final sentence says.

CHAPTER ONE

DECLARATION OF INDEPENDENCE

I s the Declaration of Independence still important? Is the United States obligated to comply with the principles in the Declaration to secure everyone's rights to life, liberty, and the pursuit of happiness?

1776

The Boston Tea Party was history (November 1773), the midnight ride of Paul Revere a distant memory (April 1775). George Washington, the commanding General of the Army was with his troops in New York.

Friday, May 10, 1776, Richard Henry Lee submitted a resolution stating that every colony should assume all powers of government independent of Great Britain. Delegates to the Continental Congress appointed by their state legislatures immediately passed the resolution.

John Adams wrote a preamble to this resolution explicitly recognizing the impossibility of reconciliation with Great Britain. Henceforth, the colonies would exercise, "all the powers of government exerted under the authority of the people of the colonies, for the preservation of internal peace, virtue, and good order, as well as the defense of their lives, liberties, and properties, against hostile invasions and cruel depredations of their enemies.[1]" After three days of debate, this too was approved on May 15th.

There would be no turning back. John Adams wrote his wife, Abigail, "I have reasons to believe that no colony which shall assume a government under the people, will give it up."[2]

May 24, General Washington began a two-day visit with Congress conveying the gravity of the situation in and around New York.

June 7, Richard Henry Lee submitted a resolution. "that these United Colonies are, and of a right ought to be, free and independent states, that they are absolved from all allegiance to the British Crown, and that all political connection between them and the state of Great Britain is, and ought to be, totally dissolved.[3]" Debate on the resolution was postponed twenty days to allow delegates from the middle colonies to obtain further instructions from state legislatures. Meanwhile, a committee of five was formed consisting of John Adams, Roger Sherman, Robert Livingston, Thomas Jefferson, and Benjamin Franklin to draft a declaration. The committee chose Jefferson to pen the initial draft.

The initial vote for independence occurred on July 1. New York abstained. South Carolina and Pennsylvania voted *no*. Delaware, with only two delegates, was split. Edward Rutledge moved to postpone the final vote one day. The next day, Pennsylvania and South Carolina switched their votes. Caesar Rodney arrived as the meeting was about to adjourn. He had ridden eighty miles, changing horses several times and looking every bit like someone who had just ridden that distance. This was not the only impediment to his appearance, however. He wore a green silk scarf over one side of his face to hide the ravages of skin cancer. His arrival gave another *yes* vote to Delaware. Twelve colonies voted in favor of independence. New York continued to abstain.

On July 3, Congress began debating Jefferson's Declaration of Independence. Jefferson remained mute as Congress debated and amended his document while Adams consistently rose to its defense. Jefferson would later write, "No man better merited than Mr. John Adams to hold a most conspicuous place in the design. He was the pillar of its support on the floor of Congress, its ablest advocate and defender against the multifarious assaults encountered."[4]

The final amendment added the phrase, "with a firm reliance on the protection of divine Providence," to the final sentence. It now reads: "And for the support of this Declaration, with a firm reliance on the protection of divine Providence, we mutually pledge to each other our lives, our fortunes, and our sacred honor."

Twelve colonies affirmed the Declaration of Independence July 4, 1776. New York continued to abstain. As word spread throughout the colonies, it was met with jubilation. News traveled slowly in those days, reaching Savannah, Georgia in August, but this did not dampen enthusiasm. However, the vote and celebrations are not the entire story.

DIVINE CONVERGENCE OF EVENTS

Who could have foreseen that Adams and Jefferson, the two men most responsible for the Declaration of Independence would outlive all who voted that fateful day? (One signer, Charles Carroll, outlived Adams and Jefferson, but he was not present when the votes were cast, July 4th, 1776. He arrived in Philadelphia after the vote but signed as an official delegate when the document returned from the printer.)

As odd as the superior longevity of Adams and Jefferson may appear, it paled in comparison to the actual date of their demise. Adams and Jefferson died on the same day, July 4th, 1826. It was the fiftieth anniversary of the Declaration of Independence. This amazing coincidence rivals any such occurrence in human history.

What are the odds that this could be a random occurrence? The probability that Adams and Jefferson would be selected out of the group of 56 signers is .00065. John Adams was 91 when he died. Lacking actuarial data from 1826, the most current actuarial tables[5] show that out of 95303 people who are 41, 2385 will die at age 91 with a probability of .0250. This must be divided by 365 to get the probability that Adams would die on July 4th of that year giving a probability of .000068563. Repeating these calculations for Jefferson who died when he was 83 gives a probability of .000094549. The probability that it would be Adams and Jefferson out of the 56 signers who would die on July 4, 1826 is .000000000004409. By contrast, the probability of having five cards dealt randomly and getting a royal flush is .000009234. You are 2,094,352 times more likely to get a royal flush after being dealt five cards than the probability that Adams and Jefferson would both die on the fiftieth anniversary of the Declaration of Independence.

The probability of Adams and Jefferson both dying on April 1st of 1826 would be the same as their death on July 4, but there would be no significance to that date. If two other founders who voted to ratify the Declaration of Independence had died on July 4th, there would be no significance to that event either. The simultaneous deaths of Adams and Jefferson on July 4, 1826 uniquely connect the Declaration of Independence with the nation's jubilee and slavery.

The commonly accepted explanation for these simultaneous deaths is that it was a random occurrence. Such a coincidence would only occur once in every 235,760,000,000 trials. Could there be another explanation?

The country and its citizens manifested a dearth of curiosity regarding this incomprehensible coincidence. Daily life continued to saturate thought life. Despite the paucity of inquisitiveness, Daniel Webster took the opportunity to pontificate on the excellence of the country in a speech delivered August 2, arguing the simultaneous deaths of Adams and Jefferson was proof "that our country, and its benefactors are objects of His care."[6] Webster presented a plausible and pleasant thought. It continued the narrative his listeners and readers were consistently hearing, and, in fact, they would have accepted none other. The truth would have had the opposite effect.

COVENANT

The final sentence of the Declaration of Independence holds the key to deciphering the enigma produced by the simultaneous deaths of Adams and Jefferson. "And for the support of this Declaration, with a firm reliance on the protection of Divine Providence, we mutually pledge to each other our lives, our fortunes, and our sacred honor." This sentence is not merely verbal flourish announcing the termination of the document. The word, "pledge," is covenant language. In exchange for the protection of Divine Providence during the Revolutionary War, it promised that the colonies would form a government based upon the principles delineated previously. "We hold these truths to be self-evident, that all men are created equal, that they are endowed by their Creator with certain unalienable rights, that among these are life, liberty, and the pursuit of happiness. That to secure these rights, governments are instituted among men, deriving their just powers from the consent of the governed." Colonists vowed to forfeit their lives, fortunes, and sacred honors if they failed to implement a government securing delineated unalienable rights.

Unfortunately, the country was not in compliance with the stated principles. By condoning slavery, the government was denying the unalienable right of liberty to slaves. Therefore, God required Adams and Jefferson to forfeit their lives to warn the nation of impending judgment.

The Bible places special significance on the fiftieth year, calling it the year of jubilee.

A jubilee shall that fiftieth year be unto you:
(LEVITICUS 25:11A)[7]

The Bible goes on to explain how the jubilee was to be celebrated.

And ye shall hallow the fiftieth year, and proclaim liberty throughout all the land unto all the inhabitants thereof: it shall be a jubilee unto you; and ye shall return every man unto his possession, and ye shall return every man unto his family.

And if he be not redeemed in these years, then he shall go out in the year of jubilee, both he, and his children with him.
(LEVITICUS 25:10,54)

Everyone was instructed to hallow the fiftieth year. One of the ways they were to do this was by freeing their slaves. When the fiftieth year of the United States had come, the slaves were not freed.

God kept Adams and Jefferson alive until the fiftieth anniversary of the ratification of our founding document to warn the country that he held it responsible for securing the right of liberty for everyone, including slaves. The fiftieth anniversary pointed to God's commandment to release slaves on the year of Jubilee, emphasizing the failure to do so. It implied that God considered our founding document a covenant.

If those thoughts were expressed, they were drowned out by the more popular version espoused by

Webster. Citizens resumed daily activities oblivious to impending judgment. However, God's warnings were ignored at their peril. The Civil War resulting from this neglect was by far the most deadly war in the nation's history. The United States suffered more deaths in that war than in all the wars this nation fought in the twentieth century.

Undoubtedly, many were focusing on the Constitution as the governing document. Prior to the Civil War, the nation had complied with the Constitution. Beyond dispute, the Constitution did not prohibit slavery. However, the Constitution did not replace or annul the Declaration.

> **Brethren, I speak after the manner of men; Though it be but a man's covenant, yet if it be confirmed, no man disannulleth, or addeth thereto**
> (GALATIANS 3:15).

The Constitution drafters did not have authority to annul the covenant after the colonies received protection from Divine Providence. The warning came in 1826 after the Constitution had been approved demonstrating that the covenant formed by the Declaration was still active.

People, no doubt, slapped Daniel Webster on his back, congratulating him on his eloquent speech, but God had not given him that message. History has proven Webster a poor prophet indeed. As we know, the nation was in imminent danger of fighting the Civil War.

God would not express divine approval of the nation only to judge it with civil war thirty-four short years later. The deaths of Adams and Jefferson foreshadowed many more deaths if the country continued to ignore its covenant.

THE BATTLE HYMN OF THE REPUBLIC

Religious leaders in the North, who did not confront the prospect of meeting freed slaves on the street who had their children sold and wives raped, were free to reflect on the meaning of the Declaration of Independence. What were the implications of God endowing unalienable rights to men?

The nation's founding document declared to the world that the fundamental responsibility of government is to protect God-given rights. Like little children promising to perform some chore in exchange for a benefit, the founding fathers sought God's help in gaining independence from England so they could establish such a government. Like little children, once independence was achieved, national leaders refused to confront the difficult question of liberty for the slaves. If God had the ability and willingness to intervene in the fledgling nation's affairs by granting independence as they had hoped, did they now anticipate that he would ignore the plight of slaves? If God grants a person liberty, what arrogant person would audaciously override God's benevolence by denying that liberty? Any competent advocate would abhor the prospect of defending such impertinent insolence before God's tribunal.

As egocentric self-focus successfully extinguished consciousness of society's collective guilt, the "**light of the world**" (John 8:12) continued to shine on the hearts of men willing to listen, revealing the foolishness of such conceit. Men began to understand that the deprivation of unalienable rights to a group of people was an insult to the God who endowed them. They began to fear that such egregious abuses and usurpations could not be borne for long.

John Brown was an abolitionist who decided the best way to free the slaves was to arm them. He and a group of men broke into the armory at Harper's Ferry to steal the armaments contained therein, but before they could escape, they were surrounded. In a speech given in court after his conviction, John Brown conveyed the motivation for his raid.

> "This court acknowledges, as I suppose, the validity of the law of God. I see a book kissed here which I suppose to be the Bible, or at least the New Testament. That teaches me that all things whatsoever I would that men should do to me, I should do even so to them. It teaches me, further, to "remember them that are in bonds, as bound with them." I endeavored to act up to that instruction. I say, I am yet too young to understand that God is any respecter of persons. I believe that to have interfered as I have done—as I have always freely admitted I have done—in behalf of His despised poor,

was not wrong, but right. Now, if it is deemed necessary that I should forfeit my life for the furtherance of the ends of justice, and mingle my blood further with the blood of my children and with the blood of millions in this slave country whose rights are disregarded by wicked, cruel, and unjust enactments—I submit, so let it be done!"[8]

Julia Ward Howe and traveling companions in a carriage delayed by passing troops beguiled the time with snatches of army songs. One commemorated the death of John Brown, "John Brown's body lies a-mouldering in the ground; His soul is marching on."[9] Reverend Clarke suggested that Howe write more uplifting lyrics to the stirring tune. Howe described how this transpired.

"I went to bed that night as usual, and slept, according to my wont, quite soundly. I awoke in the gray of the morning twilight; and as I lay waiting for the dawn, the long lines of the desired poem began to twine themselves in my mind. Having thought out all the stanzas, I said to myself, 'I must get up and write these verses down, lest I fall asleep again and forget them.' So, with a sudden effort, I sprang out of bed, and found in the dimness an old stump of a pen which I remembered to have used the day before. I scrawled the verses almost without looking at the paper."[10]

Mine eyes have seen the glory of the coming of
the Lord:
He is trampling out the vintage where the grapes
of wrath are stored;
He hath loosed the fateful lightning of His
terrible swift sword:
His truth is marching on.

I have seen Him in the watch-fires of a hundred
circling camps,
They have builded Him an altar in the evening
dews and damps;
I can read His righteous sentence by the dim and
flaring lamps:
His day is marching on.

I have read a fiery gospel writ in burnished rows
of steel:
"As ye deal with my contemners, so with you my
grace shall deal;
Let the Hero, born of woman, crush the serpent
with his heel,
Since God is marching on."

He has sounded forth the trumpet that shall
never call retreat;
He is sifting out the hearts of men before His
judgment-seat:
Oh, be swift, my soul, to answer Him! be
jubilant, my feet!
Our God is marching on.

In the beauty of the lilies Christ was born across
the sea,
With a glory in His bosom that transfigures you
and me:
As He died to make men holy, let us die to make
men free,
While God is marching on.

He is coming like the glory of the morning on
the wave,
He is Wisdom to the mighty, He is Succour to
the brave,
So the world shall be His footstool, and the soul
of Time His slave,
Our God is marching on.

The first five verses were published in the Atlantic
monthly.

Howe believed she received those words under
inspiration from God. As such, they were an accurate
message from God revealing the cause of the war as a
judgment from God for slavery and rejoicing over the
coming of that judgment.

**The righteous shall rejoice when he seeth the
vengeance**
(PSALMS 58:10A).

Everyone who has sung those words has proclaimed
and rejoiced that the Civil War was an act of divine
judgment.

The warning of the simultaneous deaths of Adams and Jefferson went unnoticed and unheeded. The citizens in 1826 remained happily ignorant of their peril and wondered at the extensive loss of life and destruction suffered a few years later. The United States complied with its covenant for the first time on December 18, 1865, with the passage of the Thirteenth Amendment prohibiting slavery. It was thirty-nine years, eight months after Adams and Jefferson forfeited their pledged lives for noncompliance as a warning of impending judgment.

PRESENT DAY APPLICATION

Prior to the Civil War, the nation had complied with the Constitution but failed to comply with the Declaration of Independence. Slave owners were willing to dissolve the union while suffering more than 600,000 deaths so they could continue sipping mint juleps in the shade while others worked their fields, prepared their food, washed their clothes, and nursed their babies. Evolution accompanied by the light of science had not eradicated blinded self-interest from the human race. If the Declaration of Independence is a covenant with God, the implications are grave indeed. It would leave us only two options. We can keep the promise our forefathers made to protect everyone's God granted rights to life and liberty or face God's righteous judgment.

CHAPTER TWO

JUBILEE PREPARATIONS

Buy the truth, and sell it not; also wisdom, and instruction, and understanding (PROVERBS 23:23).

NEW YORK POST

What thoughts occupied the people as the nation's notable anniversary approached? Newspapers help us understand the collective state of mind during the summer of 1826. The *New York Post* was published six days a week, Monday through Saturday. It was four pages long. The first page usually contained only classified ads. The second page contained any news items for that day along with additional classified ads. The third and fourth pages published more ads.

ERIE CANAL

Immediately prior to the nation's Jubilee, the city of New York celebrated the recent completion of the Erie Canal by issuing commemorative gold and silver medals. To publicize these medals, city officials sent copies to each of the surviving signers of the Declaration of Independence: John Adams, Thomas Jefferson, and Charles Carroll. These three distinguished gentlemen wrote letters of appreciation, which were published on June 24, 1826, as a means of advertising the medals. These letters reveal the popular sentiments of the day.

The people of New York exhibited understandable pride at the canal's completion which demonstrated engineering expertise, construction skill, and frontier tenacity. Adams alluded to these sentiments in his response. "I have received ... a gold medal and silver one, in commemoration of the great Canal in New York, which is the pride and wonder of the age, and deserves to be commemorated by every effort of art."

New Yorkers viewed the canal's completion as proof of continued rapid economic expansion and increasing prosperity. Carroll emphasized this theme. "The completion of the great work, uniting the western lakes with the ocean, does honor to the state of New York. May the benefits resulting from the undertaking amply reward the wise and patriotic exertions of its citizens, and perpetuate to the city of New York its growing prosperity." Jefferson foretold of future economic blessings. "This great work will immortalize the present authorities of New York, bless their descendants with wealth and prosperity." He felt these blessings flowed from wise decisions made by the founding fathers in developing the form of government which protected individual freedoms and this legacy would produce future blessings. "The surviving signers ... have the satisfaction of seeing in them, an additional manifestation of the blessings resulting from the measures in which . . . they ventured to embark their country."

CELEBRATION COVERAGE
Shortly before the nation's fiftieth birthday, announcements of plans for a celebration began to appear. The *New York Post* challenged city officials to excel in manifestations of patriotic zeal, reporting that similar efforts were transpiring throughout the nation.

Parades
The editions for Saturday, July 1, and Monday, July 3, contained eight regimental orders detailing place of assembly, line of march, and orders for issuance of ammunition for firing salutes for the National Guard. Cadets from the Military Academy at Middletown commanded by Captain Partridge and a unit called the Washington Greys from Philadelphia also marched in celebration. The Post commended the cadets, composed of 265 boys, some as young as 14, carrying all the trappings of war including a 14 pound musket, for their superior marching.

Col. Arcularious' regiment of horse military fired a national salute at the Washington military parade grounds at 7:00 AM. Major General Benedict directed the National Flag be raised at the Battery at sunrise and a national salute fired at noon. Major General Morton reviewed the Division line at 10: AM, while Brigadier General Spicer commanded a fifteen-gun salute to be fired to the right of the command and one gun to the left. The troops marched from the battery to state street, then "to Broadway, up Broadway to Maiden lane, down Maiden lane to Pearl street, through Pearl to Chatham street, down Chatham street to the Park" where they were reviewed by the Governor and dismissed.

At half past 2:00, T. L. Smith, Esq. read the Declaration of Independence. The Governor allowed citizens to view his dining rooms from 2:00 to 3:00. At 3:00 the military and citizens partook of roasted oxen and other refreshments at the intersection of McDougal and Fifth streets. At 4:00, the Corporation presented the canal medal to the son of the late Robert Fulton before invited guests proceeded to the dining room at half past 4:00.

A transparent painting decorated City Hall commemorating the Declaration of Independence. "In the rear of the Hall, the Globe, in which the United States are conspicuously delineated, will be illuminated, showing our rapid advancement among the nations of the earth. This will be done by sheets of moving fire. All the illumination will commence at dusk."[1] Rain postponed fireworks planned for the evening.

Major General Morton eloquently expounded upon the significance of the anniversary and celebrations.

> To celebrate the return of epochs important in the affairs of a nation, has the sanction of the permanent antiquity, and the period of 50 years has a high solemnity attached to it from continuance of the deity himself. No era in the affairs of the world has been of more importance than the Declaration of Independence by the

United States, it was the dawn of Freedom to mankind, and its beams are now illuminating and enlightening the world. Well may we hail this, its semi-century anniversary with joy and gratitude. When those intrepid Statesmen subscribed that immortal instrument which asserted our right in freedom and self-government, little did they imagine that in a few revolving years, their country would be surrounded by so many blessings, and would take among the nations of the earth the proud station it now occupies; while therefore the day will be devoted to demonstrations of joy, let it also be marked by a strict observance of the rules of discipline, and a prompt and ready obedience to orders.

Major General Morton evaded the moral issue of slavery by focusing on economic advancement. Unfortunately, contemporary "rules of discipline" did not require adherence to logic in the application of moral conduct.

Theaters, Gardens, and Museums
New York theaters and museums, sensing profit opportunities, offered patriotic celebrations.

TUESDAY
"LIBERTY OR DEATH"
Bunker Hill
FOURTH OF JULY.

In commemoration of the Declaration of Independence, the front of the Theatre will be brilliantly illuminated, and three Emblematical transparencies exhibited in honour of the occasion. Underneath "50th Year of Independence"

Adornments at Chatham Garden to celebrate the "national Jubilee" featured "a brilliant American Star."

Bedecking at the Vauxhall Garden commemorated the

Jubilee of the People of the United States of America, in honor of LIBERTY and INDEPENDENCE. In commemoration of an epoch dear to every true American, and every friend of liberty in any country—to impress on the youthful mind a veneration for the principles declared fifty years since on this day, and consecrated by the blood of their forefathers— to present an exhibition worthy of the taste, the wealth, and the public spirit of this metropolis, and to gratify the numerous visitors attracted by a desire to unite in the great jubilee, and witness a celebration novel to the inhabitants of other cities, no pains nor expense have been spared to render the performances and exhibitions at Vauxhall Garden on the 50th anniversary of American Independence, delightful to the stranger, and satisfactory to the citizen. … Who, that witnesses the blessings we enjoy as a people, can withhold his gratitude on the occasion and refuse to indulge "the feast of reason and the flow of soul!" Is there one such worthy the name of an American? No.

'For ne'er shall the sons of Columbia be slaves
While the earth bears a plant, or the sea rolls its waves.'

It was obvious from this statement that blacks did not qualify to be "sons of Columbia." The Vauxhall Garden promised further entertainment by offering laughing gas to the brave and a chance to observe its effects on others to the more timid.

Peale's museum provided splendid illumination from gaslights while a military band performed. The American museum celebrated the "great and glorious day" in the "most appropriate and splendid style." The Temple of Independence spared "no pains nor expense" in honoring "the greatest event of modern times, viz— *The Jubilee of the People of the United States of America.*"

Civic Celebrations

Firemen gathered and marched to celebrate the nation's grand Jubilee.

This auspicious day the Firemen of this city intend celebrating with their usual patriotism and devotion to the honor and glory of their country, with all the tokens becoming so great and joyous an occasion.

The birth day of a free and independent nation is regarded by the philanthropist with emotions most grateful; by the patriot, as a day calculated to excite in the bosoms of Freemen, feelings which can be appreciated only by such as enjoy them.

They marched to Bowery church, where they participated in a service before continuing to Green street where they were dismissed.

Trade societies raised the flag over the respective meeting places at six o'clock. At half past nine, they assembled in Canal Street. The societies consisted of tailors, cordwainers, stone cutters, bakers, coopers, leather dressers, house painters, saddlers, harness makers, chair makers, and off duty naval and military officers.

Enterprising Entrepreneurs

What would a celebration be without the ability to buy trinkets to complement and augment one's experience? A few enterprising entrepreneurs could not pass up such an opportunity. City Hall issued permits to set up booths in the Park. Jubilee medals were struck, self-sharpening pencils with extra leads ordered and parasols offered for sun protection.

Joe Bonfanti wrote a poem in eight verses advertising the many aspects of his store. The first verse is given here as an example.

THE JUBILEE; Brother Jonathan's Second Visit to JOE BONFANTI'S Fancy Store, 279 Broadway.

Tune—"Yankee Doodle."
Sal and I came down to York,
The curious things to see, sir,
For, darn it! Who the deuce would work
On FREEDOM's JUBILEE, sir?
I sold our peas, and every thing,
To market-woman aunties,
Then went with Sal, to buy a ring,
At Mister JO BONFANTI'S.
There's his number on the sign,
In Broadway, very handy,
It is Two Hundred Seventy-nine,
Sing Yankee doodle dandy.

Subsequent verses described the types of merchandise carried in Mr. Bonfanti's store. Bonfanti boasted a large inventory of jewelry, watches, and clocks. Elaborate knick-knacks that played a tune seemed to be popular including a cage with mechanical singing birds, and musical snuff boxes. In addition, there were canes, fishing rods, spy glasses, swords, pistols, dolls, paint, fragrant soaps, self-sharpening pencils, tooth-picks, silverware, gloves, et cetera. It appears Mr. Bonfanti's customers fancied clever gadgets and luxury items.

Celebration Reports

After the celebrations, the paper reported on what actually happened. Apart from the postponement of fireworks due to rain, the activities transpired as planned. The paper was able to supply additional information on the festivities by recounting speeches.

The Governor presented Colonel Wetmore's National Guard regiment with a banner displaying the insignia of New York with the following address:

> Col Wetmore, of the National Guards.
> The soldier of a free state has in addition to the chivalrie sentiment of honor so ardently cherished by military men, the elevated spirit of patriotism to direct his career and to dignify his conduct: as a component part of a Nation of free citizens, his own fame is identified with the glory of his country.
> …

Recognizing Governor Clinton as "the highest military power known to our laws," Colonel Wetmore promised that his soldiers would honorably serve under that banner.

The mayor gave the following remarks in response to an address by Colonel Doughty. He articulates the sentiments of the day and summarizes those previously expressed.

> SIR—I receive with pleasure, and reciprocate the congratulations of my fellow citizens of the ninth ward, on the anniversary of this proud day on which the fathers of our country, with steady hands and undaunted hearts, subscribed the noblest bond of union which the world has ever witnessed. That which was then a bold experiment has proved, by the experience of half a century, to be a glorious reality.

Our beloved country has prospered beyond example under the influence of our free institutions. We have proved ourselves worthy of the enjoyment of national liberty; and the world has been taught to admire the spectacle, and profit by the example of a free people, living under laws of their own adoption, and governed by rulers of their own choice.

Let then the example of those who led our nation to victory and independence encourage us to preserve, inviolate, the blessings they obtained for us: and let us, like them, be ready at all times, to pledge our lives, our fortunes, and our sacred honors, to maintain the rich inheritance which we now possess.

No circumstance is so well calculated to impress upon our minds the growing prosperity of our country as celebrating this jubilee on this spot.
...

The mayor believed that the nation's citizens proved themselves worthy of the enjoyment of national liberty. How did they prove themselves worthy? How did he define "national liberty?"

He said the world would be taught to admire the spectacle. Unfortunately, a candid world observed a nation of hypocrites declaring that God had granted everyone the unalienable right of liberty while practicing slavery.

The mayor exhorted everyone to pledge their lives, fortunes, and sacred honors to maintain their rich inheritance. He was, of course, referring to the pledge at the end of the Declaration of Independence.

The mayor felt that the celebration of the nation's Jubilee would impress upon everyone's mind the growing prosperity. The nation's attention was definitely on prosperity instead of moral failings. Mention of the Jubilee prompted no concern for the lack of these blessings among slaves.

Wishing to avoid any possibility that the Divine provider of prosperity might discover pride and arrogance in their midst and thus curtail further blessings, the Corporation invited the Right Reverend Bishop Hobart to approach the Throne of Grace to solicit continued bounty.

> Almighty God, we adore thee as the dispenser of all good, and the ruler of the Universe; and we magnify thy name for the exalted privileges with which thou has distinguished us among the nations of the earth. At thy command, a stated revolution of time was consecrated as the *jubilee of liberty* by the people of old. Accept we beseech thee the homage, which on this day that completes the 50th year of our independence as a nation, ascends from the hearts and the voices of the millions of freemen who enjoy this good land and this goodly heritage which thou hast bestowed. Under thy guardian Providence, thou Lord of Hosts, have we advanced with unparalleled rapidity in the career of glory,

prosperity, and happiness fostered by those free institutions which were planned by the wisdom and won by the valor of our fathers, some of whom still linger among us, full of years and full of honours blessed with our grateful recollections. Let the lively demonstrations of joy which mark this day as the <u>jubilee</u> of the people, be chastened with holy dignity and sobriety and accompanied with submission to the laws; so that thy favor may continue and the inestimable blessings of civil and religious freedom perpetuated to the last generations. . . . On this day, when we commemorate the great event which proved to the world that a nation who wills it, guided and fortified by Thee, shall be free, we forget not the oppressed of our race in other lands; and we implore Thee, Father of all men, in thy good time, to send them deliverance.

There was much talk of freedom and liberty in the announcements leading up to and in subsequent reporting of the nation's Jubilee celebrations. Unfortunately, slaves throughout the United States did not experience this unalienable right. In all those announcements and self-congratulatory statements, slavery was never mentioned. Some may have felt that the statements applied mostly to New York State, which contained few slaves at that time. However, the Declaration of Independence they were celebrating applied to every state, some of which contained many slaves.

Many of the articles used the term, "jubilee," and Reverend Hobart used it frequently, to display biblical knowledge while blindly ignoring the underlying meaning of the term. The only meaning retained for this word by these people was that it came around every fifty years. In retrospect, we know that God's benevolence would not continue in a land that held a portion of its population in brutal bondage?

Slaves throughout the United States would have found the Right Reverend Bishop Hobart's prayer particularly offensive. Acknowledging God as the dispenser of all good, he somehow overlooked the possibility that God would dispense good to slaves. Acknowledging God as the ruler of the Universe, he somehow overlooked God's instruction to free all slaves in the year of Jubilee. He believed he could exalt God's name while refusing to obey.

Reverend Hobart's statement, "we forget not the oppressed of our race in other lands; and we implore Thee, Father of all men, in thy good time, to send them deliverance" could have been interpreted as seeking deliverance for the slaves in other states. It could also be interpreted as seeking deliverance for white men in other cultures. In fact, the whole prayer was like that. Reverend Hobart had successfully prayed a prayer about liberty and freedom allowing both abolitionists and slave owners to hear what they wanted to hear. Both sides could believe he fully supported their position. Afterwards, he could congratulate himself on impressing his listeners with his verbal eloquence while offending no one.

How did God view Reverend Hobart's prayer? Reverend Hobart spoke in riddles and conundrums on the issue of slavery. He prayed about freedom without mentioning slavery, the overriding moral issue of his day. If Reverend Hobart truly believed that failure to obey God's instructions could lead to the loss of divine favor, he would have spoken more plainly on an issue with such potentially ruinous repercussions. As a consequence of the lack of action by the citizens of the United States, God answered Reverend Hobart's prayer for deliverance with Civil War. The consequences would have been much milder if the people had realized their responsibility to free the slaves in compliance with their pledge.

New York had been eliminating slavery gradually, and there were few slaves left in the state by that time. However, that did not eliminate all problems with the institution nor did it render New Yorkers guiltless. Census figures showed a sharp drop in the population of free blacks after 1800 which was attributed to being kidnapped and sold into slavery in the South. Two newspaper articles from this time supported that supposition.

On June 30, the *Post* reported that William Poll, a 13-year-old mulatto boy, was missing. His parents were distraught, hoping for some word concerning his location. Readers could sense the anxiety of these parents as they faced the prospect of never seeing their son again as he lived the rest of his life as a slave.

On July 1, the *Post* reprinted a story from the Philadelphia paper reporting on the condition of five kidnapped boys and one girl. One of the boys had died from a cruel beating. Three of the boys had been returned to Philadelphia. The girl, Mary Fisher, regained her freedom and chose to stay in Mississippi. The final boy was sold at Tuscaloosa and remained in the custody of his purchaser.

MARYLAND GAZETTE'S CELEBRATION COVERAGE

The *Maryland Gazette* was published weekly on Thursday. It also consisted of four pages. The first page often consisted of the transcript of a law or speech, but when this was not available, it too had classified ads. In the June 29 edition, the edition preceding July 4, the first page was devoted to a speech by Mr. Maxcy proposing a constitutional amendment for direct election of presidents. The remainder of the speech concluded one week later, July 6, 1826.

The *Maryland Gazette* did not contain any announcements of plans to celebrate the nation's fiftieth anniversary. Although the issue preceding the anniversary contained no mention of the impending fiftieth anniversary, it did include advertisements related to the celebrated document proclaiming liberty and independence.

One advertisement offered a reward for capture of a slave named Jim along with a description. The reward varied based upon the distance Jim had traveled from home. Jim must have been an elusive individual because this announcement first appeared on April 27 and ran through September 14. In a short time, Grafton Tyler removed the distance restriction offering $100 for apprehending Jim in any location.

The issue also contained notices of three sheriff's sales and one public sale listing slaves along with livestock, land, furniture, and farming utensils to be sold, "one Negro Woman named Sarah, and her female child named Celine, one Negro Girl named Susan, and one roan Horse." From this ad, we do not know if the previous master had been humane or cruel. At this point, it made little difference. Three of his slaves were going to be sold. They had no way of knowing what type of person their new master would be. The sale could separate Sarah and her daughter, Celine. They might never see each other again. Mention of the lone girl named Susan indicated that she had already been separated from her parents.

On July 6, the *Maryland Gazette* noted that Maryland and Annapolis officials made no "regular arrangements" to celebrate the nation's fiftieth birthday. Most businesses closed for the day and individual parties were cited.

The widespread patriotic fervor evident in New York was sparse in Maryland. What caused the stark contrast between the celebrations planned for the nation's fiftieth anniversary in New York City and Annapolis? Annapolis was smaller than New York but had the additional attribute of being the state capitol. The fiftieth anniversary celebrated the ratification of the Declaration of Independence. This document espoused the fundamental principle that all men are created equal with respect to God-endowed rights. The *Maryland Gazette* plainly and boldly declared that the state of Maryland ignored this supposedly self-evident truth. Maryland citizens rejoiced in the right to liberty proclaimed for them in the Declaration of Independence but an inherent right cannot be restricted to one class of people. When government determines which class of people may enjoy a privilege, the government becomes the agent dispensing that privilege, not God. In Maryland, liberty was a government-dispensed privilege.

In addition, one has to wonder if Maryland's failure to celebrate the nation's birthday was somehow related to the idea that the United States was a collection of independent states. New York celebrated July 4th as the nation's fiftieth birthday. The birthday would not be as important to people who viewed their primary allegiance to the state of Maryland instead of the United States.

When we enter into an agreement, there is no way to determine the level of commitment other parties hold. The pledge at the end of the Declaration of Independence was placed there to guarantee full commitment from all states.

Citizens in New York exuberantly celebrated the nation's Jubilee. They felt that their emotions were a natural manifestation of joy for the goodness God had bestowed upon the nation and expected citizens in the other states to share their sentiments. Their commitment to the United States was not shared.

Instead, we find the people of Annapolis, along with many others throughout the South, exhibiting minimal support.

CAPITOL CELEBRATIONS

Celebrations were planned in other cities as well. As befitting the nation's capitol, Washington, D.C. planned a grand celebration by inviting the surviving signers of the Declaration of Independence and former presidents to join in their festivities. There were only five people who met one of these two conditions, John Adams, Thomas Jefferson, Charles Carroll, James Madison, and James Monroe. Two people met both conditions, John Adams and Thomas Jefferson. As it turned out, no one was able to attend. The five worthies each expressed their regrets. John Adams and Thomas Jefferson had a more pressing obligation to attend to which could not be postponed. The New York Post reported the invitation and responses.

As the Declaration's author, Jefferson focused his response upon the principles in that document.

> May it be to the world what I believe it will be, to some parts sooner, to some later but finally to all the signal of arousing men to burst the chains under which monkish ignorance and superstition had persuaded them to bind themselves, and to assume the blessings and security of self-government. ... The general spread of the light of science has already laid open to every view

the palpable truth, that the mass of mankind has not been born with saddles on their backs, nor a favored few, booted and spurred ready to ride them legitimately, by the grace of God.

It would be the last letter Jefferson would ever write, read in his absence on the day of his death. He correctly identified the central role of the Declaration of Independence in the Jubilee celebrations noting that the true significance lay in the principles contained therein. Perhaps pride of authorship caused him to overestimate the extent and longevity of the impact of his words. Logic directed and energized by "the light of science" had proven powerless to change the attitudes of slave owners. In the days leading up to the Civil War, that light had been all but extinguished throughout the South. An old English proverb struck much closer to the truth: "There are none so blind as those who will not see. The most deluded people are those who choose to ignore what they already know."[2]

Jefferson remained active throughout his life. The convalescent period leading to his death was brief. Burwell, Jefferson's slave butler, would routinely have helped Jefferson put his boots and spurs on and take them off. Since Jefferson would die ten days after writing the above letter, he would have instructed Burwell to assist in his actual debooting and despurring following his final ride during this time period. However, he and his descendents would continue to argue that these people were their legitimate property to be used as they saw fit.

The "light of science" did not shine brightly enough for Jefferson to perceive the rights he denied to the children he fathered by slave women. This hypocrisy stripped his admonition of moral authority. Yet, Jefferson's failure to live by his expressed ideals and his dissimulation could not change the obvious meaning of our founding document nor diminish the truth of his words. None could argue convincingly that the Declaration of Independence did not require freeing the slaves.

Those reading Jefferson's words today assume he was talking about the plight of slaves when he spoke of being born with saddles on their backs. However, he associated this condition with the mass of mankind indicating a more accurate interpretation would be that he was including the lower class in any society. Slave owners who could read the Declaration of Independence and believe it did not apply to slaves would have no difficulty in avoiding all guilt from Jefferson's parting sentiments.

STATE OF THE CITIZENRY

The announcements of the impending Jubilee celebrations and subsequent recapitulations did not manifest any indication of increased importance either in placement or font size in the New York Post. Such announcements were interspersed with accounts of a coach accident and counterfeiting. The Maryland Gazette reported no official interest in celebrating the nation's fiftieth anniversary. There was no reference to any religious connection other than obligatory prayers by members of the clergy, which seemed to be the custom of the day. Most significantly, amongst the enthusiastic rejoicings over the universal liberty and increasing prosperity experienced by all freemen, there was not a word printed about the slaves who experienced none of these benefits.

New York citizens enthusiastically celebrated the Declaration principle that governments were instituted to protect their God-granted rights including life and liberty. However, the New York Post did not mention that the right of liberty was legally denied to slaves. No one seemed to notice that the document whose birth date they celebrated proclaimed an unalienable right to liberty for all. New York Post articles frequently mentioned the fact that the nation was celebrating its Jubilee. However, they never mentioned the biblical instruction to free the slaves. The slaves themselves connected the Jubilee with their freedom. When they spoke of a future time when they would be free they often spoke of experiencing their Jubilee.

Citizens attributed their rapid growth and increasing prosperity to their wisdom which resulted in their form of government. They focused on the benefits these rights and institutions provided to themselves ignoring any accompanying responsibility. Their increasing prosperity led them to believe that God was blessing them and, therefore, he must be pleased with them. Maryland citizens somehow may have sensed that abolitionists would make extensive use of the Declaration to argue that they should free their slaves.

Their celebrations were more subdued. All were about to learn of an event occurring on their anniversary that could have changed everyone's perceptions if it had been properly explained and understood.

supposing that gain is godliness: from such withdraw thyself
(1 TIMOTHY 6:5B).

CHAPTER THREE

DEATHS OF ADAMS AND JEFFERSON

When planning for tomorrow, we assume that it will look much like today. Once in a while, a dramatic event causes everyone to realize that tomorrow and all subsequent days will be fundamentally different than yesterday. Such an event occurred when terrorists flew planes into the Twin Towers on September 11, 2001. Such an event also occurred July 4, 1826, but no one recognized its significance at that time, and no one recognizes it still.

NEW YORK POST COVERAGE

The first mention of the death of Adams in the *New York Post* appeared on July 7, 1826. It reported actions by the Massachusetts Governor to honor the death. The funeral took place at three o'clock the same day the announcement appeared. The governor ordered minute guns to be fired from the Massachusetts State House during the funeral, from noon until one o'clock on the 5th, when the notice was received at Quincy, Massachusetts, Adam's home.

On July 8th, the *Post* learned that Jefferson had also died on the 4th.

The circumstance attending the death of these two venerable old men, both formerly presidents of the United States, both signers of the Declaration of Independence, both called away on the same day, and that, too, the fiftieth anniversary of the day when that instrument was signed—all form a coincidence of which the world scarcely produces a parallel. It cannot be doubted, that if the choice had been with them, they would have fixed on the very day for the termination of their mortal careers which an all wise God has seen fit to choose for this solemn purpose.

On July 10, the *Post* reported similar sentiments expressed in the Philadelphia *National Gazette* on the same day.

The dissolution of two of the three survivors of the magnanimous men who raised the perpetual standard of American sovereignty, within the same day, being that which closed the fiftieth year since their glorious deed, makes a coincidence so striking that it has immediately affected every person, and in a former age would have been deemed ominous, or at least a special dispensation of Divine Providence.

The *New York Post* intimates that God orchestrated this improbable event. The paper does not explain God's reason for arranging such a result. If God did arrange the simultaneous deaths of Adams and Jefferson, surely it would be vitally important to understand God's purpose. The *Post* offers no explanation, does not pose the question, and there is no indication that the public considered it important enough to pursue. The Philadelphia *National Gazette* proclaimed that such an event "would have been deemed ominous" in a former age. However, not even this incredible coincidence could distract citizens of that day from their bulldog, locked-jaw focus on financial prosperity.

MARYLAND GAZETTE COVERAGE

News of the simultaneous deaths of Adams and Jefferson was not published in the *Maryland Gazette* until July 13th. While there were no officially sanctioned or public celebrations of the fiftieth anniversary of the United States in Annapolis, the *Maryland Gazette* provided extensive coverage of the deaths of these two founding fathers.

Jefferson died a few minutes before 1 o'clock of diarrhea while the Declaration of Independence was being read in Charlottesville. He had been confined to his bed for a week. On Monday, July 3, he asked about the date and made known his desire to "breathe the air of the 50th Anniversary." The *Gazette* assured its readers that he died calmly with "all the equanimity of a sage."

The *Gazette* announced Jefferson's death while extolling his accomplishments and eulogizing his character. In Virginia, the House of Delegates, the Senate Chamber and the Executive Chamber were hung in mourning, the Guard House Bell tolled and minute guns fired throughout the day. The national government expressed similar sentiments.

The *Gazette* continued with the announcement of Adam's death, commenting on the coincidence. "Singular, indeed, was the coincidence, that they should both have been summoned from time to eternity, on that memorable anniversary which is hallowed as the birth-day of American freedom, and which fifty years ago, they both assisted in proclaiming to the world, by affixing their signatures to the inviolate charter of our liberties." The funeral for Adams was held in his hometown of Quincy. Jefferson was buried in the cemetery at Monticello.

Jefferson and Adams were the last two survivors who had voted to ratify the Declaration of Independence. One signer of the Declaration, Charles Carroll, survived them, but he had not been present on July 4th when the Declaration was ratified. Because Carroll was from Maryland, the Gazette felt it necessary to explain this circumstance which it did in articles on July 20th and August 3.

The articles were inconsistent. The most likely explanation was that, being Catholic, the Continental Congress selected Carroll for a secret mission to Canada in an attempt to persuade the Catholics in the Canadian provinces to join in the rebellion against England. Upon his return, he was elected to Congress and upon taking his seat on the 18th, signed the Declaration.

There was an obvious misconception about the signing of the Declaration of Independence in the newspaper articles. The Declaration of Independence was debated and ratified on July 4th. The document, as amended, was then sent to the printer. When it returned, the delegates filed in to sign it as their schedules permitted. All the signatures affixed to the final document were placed there after July 4th[th]. Although Charles Carroll survived Adams and Jefferson as the last surviving signer of the Declaration of Independence, he was not present on July 4th when it was ratified. With the deaths of Adams and Jefferson, all who had voted for ratification were deceased.

NATIONAL DELUSION

The founding fathers felt they fulfilled their pledge by supporting the Revolutionary War. However, they did not pledge to fight the war. They pledged to form a government based upon the principle that God endows everybody with an equal set of rights including life and liberty. God gave the Israelites fifty years to free their slaves. When America's Jubilee arrived marking the fifty-year anniversary, only two men who voted for ratification of the Declaration remained. They died on that day as a sign from God that citizens had not kept their pledge.

Despite the national disgrace of slavery, the idea of God warning the nation of impending judgment via the simultaneous deaths of Adams and Jefferson on the nation's Jubilee was never mentioned. Daniel Webster presented a far more appealing hypothesis that this was a sign of divine favor. Webster never explained why God would use the death of the two individuals most responsible for the Declaration of Independence to proclaim divine approval. He never explained how the nation's Jubilee related to divine approval rather than the requirement to free the slaves. Unfortunately, the people were not searching for logical explanations. Instead, they searched for an interpretation of events that would make them feel good about themselves and their situation.

The majority of citizens did not yet consider slavery a national disgrace. They had lived with and experienced slavery to some extent all their lives. They were desensitized. It began in 1619 in the settlement at Jamestown over 200 years before. They were unaware of any divine judgments during that time. Why would God judge the nation now? The nation's Jubilee was a natural time to pause and consider the morality of this institution, but people were more interested in celebrating their increasing prosperity.

However, the spiritual atmosphere in the land had changed with the ratification of the Declaration of Independence. This change was subtle and undiscerned by the populace at large who did not recognize God's voice. However, the founding fathers had signed the pledge for their respective colonies to form a government based upon the principle that God had granted everyone the unalienable rights of life and liberty in exchange for divine favor in gaining independence. Could a nation pledge to perform a duty in exchange for divine favor and then renege on its promise without experiencing divine judgment?

Citizens resumed daily activities oblivious to impending judgment. However, ignoring God's warnings because the message is unpopular or self-interest absorbs rational thought is foolhardy. By failing to heed this warning, the citizens of that day sowed the seeds of future judgment. They felt they could support or tolerate the continued existence of slavery without sacrificing the blessings of God. They were tragically mistaken. Meanwhile, the slavery debate began to heat up with much of the argument focused on the Declaration of Independence.

CHAPTER FOUR

DECLARATION DEBATE

He, that being often reproved hardeneth his neck, shall suddenly be destroyed, and that without remedy

(PROVERBS 29:1).

The concept of rights was widely discussed and debated prior to the Revolutionary War. Some philosophers divided rights into two categories, natural rights and legal rights. Natural rights were those inherent to an individual. Legal rights were those bestowed by government. Other philosophers, noting that rights bestowed by government could be rescinded by government, felt that legal rights were not rights at all but government favor.

Colonists initially argued they had the legal rights of Englishmen. However, when they pressed their claim to rights with the King of England, this argument lacked coherence and effectiveness. There was something unseemly about crawling hat-in-hand to the English monarch requesting that he honor their rights as Englishmen. As the English monarch, King George had at least some authority in determining the extent of

English rights. The debate forced colonists to develop and expand their understanding of rights. A right is something inherent to a person. It was illogical to beg for something a person inherently possessed.

Jefferson realized that the colonist's ability to obtain redress for grievances was hindered by faulty logic. For Jefferson's claim to succeed, he would have to argue that colonists' rights came from a source the English monarch was obligated to respect. The Declaration of Independence asserted that God was the only one who can bestow rights which could never be rescinded although they could be forfeited by wicked acts or abrogated by immoral authority.

The Declaration was widely held as a profound statement on the rights of man. However, there were unintended consequences. When colonists had argued for rights as Englishmen, blacks were logically excluded, but many felt blacks could no longer be excluded if rights originated from God. The Bible declared God was no respecter of persons. The Declaration declared that all men were created equal with respect to God-endowed rights. Would God create a race of people, lacking basic rights? If Jefferson's assertion that rights come from God was correct, was it possible for men to be endowed with rights their neighbors lack?

In delineating natural rights, earlier philosophers such as John Locke had named life, liberty, and property. Adams used this list in his preamble to Lee's resolution approved May 15th. In accordance with other philosophers, Jefferson exchanged the right of property for the right to pursue happiness. Whether or not Jefferson accepted the right to pursue happiness as superior in a philosophical sense to the right of property, there can be no doubt that it had wider application. Everyone could pursue happiness but wealthy plantation owners like Jefferson participated in the right of property more than frontier laborers. The shift in emphasis from colonial aristocrats to plebeian peasants appears to be a shrewd marketing ploy. The brunt of war's dangers and depravations would be borne by men with limited property. Perhaps Jefferson chose the right to pursue happiness to demonstrate more clearly how the long train of abuses and usurpations violated God-endowed rights. Whatever the reason, the adjustment to appeal to poorer citizens had significant impact on the poorest in the land. By failing to mention the right of property, Jefferson prevented slavery advocates from referring to the Declaration of Independence to defend their right to own slaves in future slavery debates.

Men viewed the concepts enshrined in the Declaration differently. Southerners viewed them as a proposition to debate and reject. They rejected the idea of inalienable rights while believing they could retain such rights for themselves. Abolitionists viewed the Declaration's concepts as self-evident truths. The simultaneous deaths of Adams and Jefferson on the nation's Jubilee coupled with the final sentence indicated the Declaration of Independence was a vow to God. The consequences of this debate were vital. The differing beliefs lead to vastly different courses.

DECLARATION IN SLAVERY DEBATE

The concise, direct expostulation of God granted rights in the Declaration of Independence made it the preeminent source in the slavery debate. William Lloyd Garrison was a leader of the abolitionist movement as editor of "*The Liberator*," a weekly newspaper. His arguments were based upon the Bible and the Declaration of Independence. "Lundy personified the visionary 'new race of editors' to which Garrison aspired. … Their faiths stood upon the same twin rocks—the Bible and the Declaration of Independence."[1] "'We plant ourselves upon the truths of Divine Revelation and the Declaration of Independence as upon the EVERLASTING ROCK.'"[2]

THE ABOLITIONIST

Garrison expressed these sentiments in an address delivered in the Broadway Tabernacle, New York, February 14, 1854.

> I am a believer in that portion of the Declaration of American Independence in which it is set forth, as among self-evident truths, 'that all men are created equal; that they are endowed by their Creator with certain inalienable rights; that among these are life, liberty, and the pursuit of happiness.' Hence, I am an abolitionist.[3]

The first issue of *The Liberator* published January 1st, 1831, Volume 1, Number 1, referenced the Declaration of Independence in the three articles on the first page.

The Slave Trade in the Capital: It is well, perhaps the American people should know, that while we reiterate our boasts of liberty in the ears of the nations, and send back across the Atlantic our shouts of joy at the triumph of liberty in France, we ourselves are busily engaged in the work of oppression. Yes, let it be known to the citizens of America, that at the very time when the procession which contained the President of the United States and his Cabinet was marching in triumph to the Capitol, to celebrate the victory of the French people over their oppressors, another kind of procession was marching another way, and that consisted of colored human beings, handcuffed in pairs, and driven along by what had the appearance of a man on a horse! A similar scene was repeated on Saturday last; a drove consisting of males and females chained in couples, starting from Roby's tavern on foot, for Alexandria, where, with others, they are to embark on board a slave-ship in waiting to convey them to the South. . . .

Oh patriotism! Where is thy indignation? Oh philanthropy! Where is thy grief? OH SHAME, WHERE IS THY BLUSH? Well may the generous and noble minded O'Connell say of the American citizen, 'I tell him he is a hypocrite. Look at the stain in your star-spangled standard that was never struck down in battle. I turn from the Declaration of American Independence, and I tell him that he has declared to God and man a lie, and before God and man I arraign him as a hypocrite.'

Two years later, December of 1833, Garrison wrote the *"Declaration of Sentiments of the American Anti-Slavery Society."* He began this document by referring to those who 57 years earlier had declared that God had endowed everyone with the inalienable rights of "life, LIBERTY, and the pursuit of happiness." (Capitals in the original.)[4]

SOUTHERN RESPONSE

On August 16, 1818, Jacob Gruber, a Methodist minister, spoke at a camp meeting at Hagerstown, Maryland, on national sins. After discussing other sins, he progressed to the subject of slavery. "We live in a free country; and that all men are created equal and have inalienable rights, such as life, liberty, and the pursuit of happiness, we hold as inalienable truths. But there are slaves in our country, and their sweat and blood, and tears declare them such."[5]

About twenty-six hundred white people were in the audience, and over four hundred Negroes were on the outskirts of the crowd. The bold evangelist attacked the cruel and inhumane institution of slavery as being inconsistent with the Declaration of Independence. Consequently, offended slave owners obtained a grand jury indictment for attempting to incite slaves to rebellion.

Roger Taney was counsel for the defense. He would later become Chief Justice of the Supreme Court where he would author the Dred Scott decision. However, on this day he successfully defended his client's right to refer to the nation's founding document.

> Any man has a right to publish his opinions on that subject [slavery] whenever he pleases. … Mr. Gruber did quote the language of our great act of national independence, and insisted on the principles contained in that venerated instrument. … Until the time shall come when we can point without a blush, to the language of the Declaration of Independence, every friend of humanity will seek to lighten the galling chain of slavery, and better, to the utmost of his power, the wretched condition of the slave.[6]

Gruber could not reference the founding document of the country in Maryland without being charged with a crime. He was found to be not guilty only after undergoing the expense and inconvenience of a trial. By such actions, Southerners discouraged anyone from depicting the depravity of slavery.

Such arguments convinced Abraham Lincoln of the correctness and vital importance of the Declaration of Independence. He expressed his convictions in an address at Independence Hall in Philadelphia on February 22, 1861. "I have never had a feeling politically that did not spring from the sentiments embodied in the Declaration of Independence."[7]

As debate progressed, religious and political leaders throughout the South grasped and acknowledged the truth that slavery was incompatible with the Declaration of Independence. They stopped blushing at our founding document and began attacking it. William A. Smith, president of Randolph and Macon College "assailed Jefferson and the doctrine of equality, as did virtually all the southern divines, and upheld the principle of slavery in the abstract."[8] Presbyterian minister Frederick A. Ross, author of *Slavery Ordained of God*, stated, "'Moses and Paul were not moved by the Holy Ghost to sanction the philosophy of Thomas Jefferson.'"[9] "John C. Calhoun refuted the Declaration's central claim that 'all men are created equal' by observing that 'all men are not created. According to the Bible, only two—a man and a woman—ever were—and of these one was pronounced subordinate to the other. All others have come into the world by being born, and in no sense . . . either free or equal.'"[10] Calhoun's theology was faulty. The Bible also uses the word, "made," to describe God's act of creating, the same word that is used in Genesis 9:6.

> **Whoso sheddeth man's blood, by man shall his blood be shed: for in the image of God made he man**
> (GENESIS 9:6).

According to Calhoun's argument, we could safely murder anyone except Adam and Eve.

Edmund Ruffin, President of the Virginia State Agricultural Society, began an article addressing the African colonization effort in Liberia with a discussion of natural rights. These rights formed the foundation of the Declaration of Independence. Referring to the Declaration, Ruffin argued that small minds had turned "frothy rhetoric" into "the citadel of defence for the new and zealous party of abolitionists of negro slavery."[11]

James Henry Hammond in his *Letter to an English Abolitionist*, after a theological defense of slavery, dismissed the principles of the Declaration without justification. "I repudiate, as ridiculously absurd, that much lauded but nowhere accredited dogma of Mr. Jefferson, that 'all men are born equal.'"[12] In his dismissal, he could not even quote the Declaration accurately for the Jefferson argued that "all men are created equal," not "born equal." This subtle change eliminated the agency of God. If we agree that men are created, we simultaneously agree there must be a creator. The belief that God had endowed slaves with the right of liberty motivated abolitionists to defend that right.

John Quincy Adams recorded in his journal for February 14th, 1838, events in the House of Representatives as he presented petitions to that organization.

> I said that in another part of the Capitol it had been threatened [by a senator] that if a Northern abolitionist should go to South Carolina and utter a principle of the Declaration of Independence— here a loud cry of order— order— burst forth, in which the Speaker yelled among the loudest—I waited till it subsided and

then resumed; that if they could catch him they would hang him.[13]

The House had passed a gag rule prohibiting representatives from speaking about petitions on the subject of slavery. Adams opposed this rule as being unconstitutional, prohibiting the right of petition guaranteed in the First Amendment. He also opposed slavery. By this point, Southern representatives considered a reference to the Declaration as equivalent to mentioning slavery in violation of their gag rule. John Quincy Adams' father, John Adams, was second only to Thomas Jefferson in his contributions to the nation's founding document. The outcry from Southerners at the mention of this document must have struck him as profoundly significant. They had rejected the underlying principles of this document because those principles rejected the idea that God approved of slavery. Southerners had long realized that slavery was incompatible with this document. Support of slavery required rejecting the Declaration.

The slavery debate focused on the word, "liberty" in the Declaration of Independence. Beyond all dispute, liberty was denied to slaves and the Declaration declared without apology that liberty was an inalienable right endowed by God. To defend slavery, Calhoun realized that he had to confront the idea that everyone was entitled to liberty. He developed a theory of government to explain why liberty was not an inalienable right stating, "it is a great and dangerous error to suppose that all people are equally entitled to liberty."[14] Southerners could believe Calhoun or the Declaration but not both. The Declaration said all were endowed with an equal right to liberty.

DRED SCOTT DECISION

Slave Dred Scott sued for his freedom based upon several years of residence in states where slavery was illegal. The case reached the Supreme Court where the court ruled that Scott could not sue in federal court since slaves were not citizens. This ruling raised additional questions concerning the rights of mixed children, which the court ignored.

Normally, the Supreme Court decision would have ended once the court determined that Dred Scott had no standing to bring suit, but Chief Justice Taney, in light of the slavery debate, felt compelled to continue the defense of his opinion as it related to the Declaration of Independence by opining negatively on the qualifications of blacks in general.

> They were at that time considered as a subordinate and inferior class of beings, who had been subjugated by the dominant race, and, whether emancipated or not, yet remained subject to their authority, and had no rights or privileges but such as those who held the power and the Government might choose to grant them.

Taney's reference to rights responded to the Declaration's proclamation that everyone had equal rights. He continued, stating facts that were not true in every situation.

> In the opinion of the court, the legislation and histories of the times, and the language used in the Declaration of Independence, show, that neither the class of persons who had been imported as slaves, nor their descendants, whether they had become free or not, were then acknowledged as a part of the people, nor intended to be included in the general words used in that memorable instrument.

There were free Negroes during the Revolutionary War. One of the first persons to die during the Revolutionary War was black. There was no reason to think that they were not considered citizens for a citizen of any state when the Constitution was ratified would have been considered a citizen of the United States.

Taney asserted the Declaration of Independence did not have slaves in mind when it proclaimed that all men were created equal and concluded that slaves, therefore, possessed no unalienable right to liberty. He drew this conclusion from its implementation, not the words used.

> It is difficult at this day to realize the state of public opinion in relation to that unfortunate race, which prevailed in the civilized and enlightened portions of the world at the time of the Declaration of Independence, and when the

Constitution of the United States was framed and adopted. . . .

They had for more than a century before been regarded as beings of an inferior order, and altogether unfit to associate with the white race, either in social or political relations; and so far inferior, that they had no rights which the white man was bound to respect; and that the negro might justly and lawfully be reduced to slavery for his benefit. He was bought and sold, and treated as an ordinary article of merchandise and traffic, whenever a profit could be made by it.

Arguing that English words had not changed their meaning in the Declaration of Independence and that the truths remained self-evident, abolitionists continued to use this document in their condemnation of slavery.

Taney framed an argument based on a premise that was verifiably false. "And in no nation was this opinion more firmly fixed or more uniformly acted upon than by the English Government and English people." There were many who held an opposing opinion during the conventions debating the Declaration of Independence and the Constitution. They compromised their beliefs because they were convinced that these documents must receive unanimous approval to deny Britain access to this continent. The first London edition of the Declaration of Independence was published by *The Gentleman's Magazine* in August 1776. A month later a response was published pointing out the discrepancy between the ideals stated in that document and the institution of slavery.

> We hold (they say) these truths to be self-evident: That all men are created equal. In what are they created equal? Is it in size, understanding, figure, moral or civil accomplishments, or situation of life? Every plough-man knows that they are not created equal in any of these. … That every man hath an unalienable right to liberty; and here the words, as it happens, are not nonsense, but they are not true: slaves there are in America, and where there are slaves, there liberty is alienated.[15]

Obviously, English people did not hold a uniform view that negroes might justly and lawfully be reduced to slavery for their benefit.

> The language of the Declaration of Independence is equally conclusive:
> It begins by declaring that, 'when in the course of human events it becomes necessary for one people to dissolve the political bands which have connected them with another, and to assume among the powers of the earth the separate and equal station to which the laws of nature and nature's God entitle them, a decent respect for the opinions of mankind requires that they should declare the causes which impel them to the separation.'

It then proceeds to say: 'We hold these truths to be self-evident: that all men are created equal; that they are endowed by their Creator with certain unalienable rights; that among them is life, liberty, and the pursuit of happiness; that to secure these rights, Governments are instituted, deriving their just powers from the consent of the governed.'

The general words above quoted would seem to embrace the whole human family, and if they were used in a similar instrument at this day would be so understood. But it is too clear for dispute, that the enslaved African race were not intended to be included, and formed no part of the people who framed and adopted this declaration; for if the language, as understood in that day, would embrace them, the conduct of the distinguished men who framed the Declaration of Independence would have been utterly and flagrantly inconsistent with the principles they asserted; and instead of the sympathy of mankind, to which they so confidently appealed, they would have deserved and received universal rebuke and reprobation.

Taney offered the country a choice. Literal interpretation of the Declaration required universal rebuke and reprobation for the founding fathers. Logic and morality were in one hand and the reputation of the founding fathers in the other.

Taney continued to argue that English words must be understood in a different way in this document based upon the way it was implemented.

> Yet the men who framed this declaration were great men high in literary acquirements high in their sense of honor, and incapable of asserting principles inconsistent with those on which they were acting.

Taney implies that learned men cannot be hypocrites. The history of slavery and the slavery debate have proven beyond any doubt that learning and hypocrisy are not mutually exclusive.

Taney continued to overstate his authority as Supreme Court Chief Justice assuming he could rewrite history and the way people understood words.

> They perfectly understood the meaning of the language they used, and how it would be understood by others; and they knew that it would not in any part of the civilized world be supposed to embrace the negro race, which, by common consent, had been excluded from civilized Governments and the family of nations, and doomed to slavery. They spoke and acted according to the then established doctrines and principles, and in the ordinary language of the day, and no one misunderstood them. The unhappy black race were separated from the white by indelible marks, and laws long before

established, and were never thought of or spoken of except as property, and when the claims of the owner or the profit of the trader were supposed to need protection.

First of all, the words were not universally understood as Taney asserted. Taney argued that the negro race was inferior concluding that it was morally right to enslave them. Even though the words of the Declaration declared that all men were created equal, experience teaches us that this is absurd. Humans are unique. The Declaration made the point that everyone was equal with respect to God endowed rights. The rights were not earned or merited but endowed. Therefore, any argument about the superiority of inferiority of one race over the other was irrelevant. Taney argued that everyone understood at the time that the Declaration would never be interpreted to include blacks at the very time he was disputing abolitionists on that point.

By Taney's time, the races were no longer separated by "indelible marks." Some children born of white fathers and slave mothers were mostly white by this time and could pass for white.

Taney's interpretation of the Declaration of Independence was illogical in another respect. The document declared that God endowed everyone with an equal set of rights. If this was true, then how men at the time interpreted those words was irrelevant. If God endowed rights, God determined who received those rights, and he did not require or seek the counsel or permission of men.

The Dred Scott decision was an attempt by one of the most learned Southern minds, the Supreme Court Chief Justice, to argue that the Declaration of Independence did not claim that blacks possessed unalienable rights. He could make whatever argument he chose. It mattered not. His words became the law of the land by fiat. However, his words did not alter God's opinion. If the Declaration of Independence was a covenant with God and that covenant included blacks, their exclusion would result in harsh judgment for those who arrogantly ignored proclaimed, self-evident truths.

LOGICAL RESPONSE

Beyond dispute, the principles boldly and clearly stated in the Declaration of Independence were incompatible with slavery. The only question was whether these principles were true. Southerners debated and judged the idea of God endowing mankind with unalienable rights. Realizing that acceptance of this idea would require freeing their slaves; they became hostile to Jefferson and the Declaration. They either attacked the ideas or ignored them arguing instead that they had the right to secede. There is no indication that they considered the cost if they were mistaken despite warnings.

Congressman Francis James introduced a petition in the House of Representatives which would repeal any laws in the District of Columbia or the territories that did not comply with the Declaration of Independence or the Golden rule. Southern congressmen immediately killed this petition implicitly admitting that slavery violated both. In addition, they were announcing that they approved of their peculiar institution and had no intention of complying with either the Declaration or the Golden rule.[16]

DECLARATION AS COVENANT

The Declaration of Independence can be taken three ways. It can be viewed as flawed philosophy, accurate philosophy or a covenant with God. If it is a covenant, that puts it in a whole different realm. Men can no longer debate or judge it. They can only comply with the covenant or face judgment.

By refusing to acknowledge the principles in the Declaration of Independence, citizens in the South felt they could annul it, choosing instead war with the rest of the country. They thought they could ignore truth thereby freeing themselves from the requirement to recognize the slave's unalienable right of liberty. They lacked the authority to annul the covenant. Unknowingly, Southerners entered into a war against God as God's truth was marching on.

CHAPTER FIVE

HONOR

A good name is rather to be chosen than great riches, and loving favour rather than silver and gold

(PROVERBS 22:1).

DECLARATION DISHONORED

As the slavery debate progressed, it became obvious that Southern society's support of slavery could not be reconciled with the Declaration of Independence or biblical principles. Abolitionists arguing from these documents labeled Southerners immoral hypocrites.

The desire for a positive self-image motivated Southerners to adopt a moral code they could reconcile with their conduct. English heritage had given the colonies an understanding of honor society as portrayed in romance novels. The founding fathers were familiar with these cultural norms. They affected their beliefs and conduct. As Northern culture migrated toward conduct governed by the Declaration of Independence and the Bible, the South drifted towards ideals depicted in novels.[1] Sir Walter Scott portrayed a society composed of gallant gentlemen and refined ladies. This life style fit more closely with Southern experiences than those taught in the Bible. And so, Southerners put down their Bibles and picked up their "Sir Walter Scotts." "The Southern fascination for Scott's romances was so great that Mark Twain later called it the 'Sir Walter disease.'"[2]

The honor culture emphasized a person's responsibility to tell the truth. To accuse another of lying directly attacked the person's honor and would be defended in the upper class by fighting a duel. Theoretically, the duel demonstrated that the antagonists valued honor more than their lives. The fallacy with this philosophy was that fighting a duel had no relationship to ethical conduct. The most unrepentant liar could fight duels. Dueling only prevented careful observers from publishing the names of liars. Ultimately, the only accurate measure of honor was observation of how well people respected the truth.

Another measure of honor was the way people kept their word. Thomas Jefferson's grandson, Thomas Jefferson Randolph, was the executor of Jefferson's estate. Unfortunately, Jefferson's debts exceeded his assets. As executor and heir, Randolph felt obligated to pay off his grandfather's debts, which took him a number of years. Southern culture expected and promoted such conduct.

Although Randolph felt obligated to honor his grandfather's financial obligations, he exhibited no awareness of the pledge Jefferson made in the Declaration of Independence. The South's honor society developed as a result of slavery and would do nothing that endangered the status quo of that institution.

The majority of Southern citizens would have found nothing honorable in supporting the principles of that document as guaranteed by the pledge signed by the founding fathers as they represented their respective colonies. Thus, Southern society honored most pledges while vehemently ignoring the one in the country's founding document.

The final sentence of the Declaration of Independence illustrates the importance placed upon honor by the founding fathers who pledged their lives, fortunes, and sacred honor. The placement of the word "honor" and the modifier "sacred" emphasized that these men valued honor more than life and fortune.

The founding fathers had promised God they would form a government guaranteeing life and liberty to everyone. Although all the founding fathers made this promise, not all kept their word. While some worked toward this end by opposing slavery, others supported slavery seemingly oblivious to the obvious truth that they were breaking their oath to God. The Declaration that bore their signatures was transmitted throughout the world for all to see as the reason for fighting the Revolutionary War. Those promoting slavery were blatantly lying before the whole world and became offended whenever anyone pointed this out.

The word "honor" can refer to a person's reputation or ethical conduct. Theoretically, ethical conduct resulted in good reputations. Ultimately, the primary objective of Southern society was the protection and promotion of slavery. Whenever, the ideals of their honor society came in conflict with slavery, ideals yielded.

Ultimately, slavery was found to be inconsistent with the ideals of an honor society. Slavery forced Southerners to lie about the conditions of slaves and ignore the pledge of the founding fathers. Ironically, the founding fathers had pledged their sacred honor that the country would abide by the principles in the Declaration. It proved impossible for anyone to oppose those principles and maintain his or her honor.

AVOIDING AGITATION

Abolitionists viewed slavery as the greatest evil facing the nation. Others viewed the possibility of Civil War as the greatest evil. This second group viewed abolitionist literature as a dangerous, unprovoked agitation. They realized that such attacks on a personal level invariably resulted in a challenge to a duel of honor in Southern states. Familiar with Southern culture, these people warned of fatal consequences.

In defense of their honor, Southerners demanded that others relinquish their right of expression. John C. Calhoun predicted the eventual secession of the South in his last speech to the Senate on March 4, 1850. It began by naming the underlying cause. "I have, Senators, believed from the first that the agitation of the subject of slavery would, if not prevented by some timely and effective measure, end in disunion."[3] He developed this argument throughout. "Is it, then, not certain, that if something is not done to arrest it, the South will be forced to choose between abolition and secession?"⁴ Since Calhoun could not challenge the publishers of abolitionist literature to a duel, he threatened the national equivalence, secession and Civil War, instead. This threat accorded with Southern cultural norms and was liable to the same fallacy that dueling suffered. The ultimate goal of secession was the continued disregarding of the country's pledge. All who fought to protect and promote slavery did indeed forfeit their sacred honor, and they were not even aware of it.

The attitude and conduct nurtured and promoted by this emphasis on honor is illustrated by an article published in the *Richmond Enquirer*:

> If the people of the North would cease to hurl thunderbolts at us from their pulpits, to fulminate firebrands into our society through their press, to attempt to intercept us in every territory, to defraud and to force us out of our rights; if in other words, they would render unto Caesar the things that are Caesar's; concede to us equality in the Union, offer no illegal and unjust obstruction to the extension of our institutions, if they would let us alone and leave slavery to the states, and to the same protection and privileges enjoyed by all other property under the Constitution, the agitation of the question would come to an end on the instant. The trouble would cease simultaneously with the cause that produced it. But, as long as they empty their vials of wrath upon our heads, ours must be

emptied on theirs. If they propagate calumnies, we must refute them. If they incite their people to hate and assault the South, we must incite our people to reciprocate the hatred, and repel the attacks. If they smite us on the cheek, we cannot and will not turn the other to them too. If there is a danger in agitation, there is still more danger in supineness and submission.[5]

This article alluded to Jesus' instruction to render unto Caesar the things that are Caesar's but left out the more important admonition to render unto God the things that are God's. Abolitionists opposed slavery, not on civil grounds, but on moral grounds. Abolitionists were not a majority in the North, yet Southerners blamed everyone in the North for not silencing them.

The president of the Confederacy, Jefferson Davis, reminded Confederates at the beginning of the war how some Northern representatives (who were always in the minority) had offended Southern honor.

Emboldened by success, on the theatre of agitation and aggression against the clearly expressed constitutional rights of the Congress, Senators and Representatives were sent to the common councils of the nation, whose chief title to this distinction consisted in the display of a spirit of ultra fanaticism, and whose business was not to promote the general welfare, or ensure domestic tranquillity—but to awaken the bitterest hatred against the citizens of sister States by violent denunciations of their institutions.[6]

Years after the war, Southerners continued to expound on the superiority of Southern antebellum culture resulting from their emphasis on the ideals of honor depicted in Romance literature.

> On one side of the conflict was the South, led by the descendants of the Cavaliers, who with all their faults, had inherited from a long line of ancestors a manly contempt for moral littleness, a high sense of honor, a lofty regard for plighted faith, a strong tendency to conservatism, a profound respect for law and order, and an unfaltering loyalty to constitutional government. Against the South was arrayed the power of the North, dominated by the spirit of Puritanism, which, with all its virtues, has ever been characterized by the pharisaism which worships itself, and is unable to perceive any goodness apart from itself, which has ever arrogantly held its ideas, its interests, and its will higher than fundamental law and covenanted obligations, which as always 'lived and moved and had its being' in rebellion against constituted authority."[7]

Southern arguments implied abolitionists attacked Southerners from some malicious motive. Abolitionists' arguments were not motivated by animosity but by moral principle. Southerners, unable to address the moral issue, responded with overblown bombast.

Despite the first amendment, slavery advocates successfully denied freedom of speech and freedom of the press to some abolitionists. In 1837, Reverend Lovejoy obtained a printing press with which he intended to publish anti-slavery material. On November 6th, the press was moved into an upper room in Alton, Illinois. The next evening, a pro-slavery mob formed setting fire to the building containing the press and killing Lovejoy. Alton, Illinois lay across the Mississippi River from slave country. On that night, the sentiments of Calhoun and his fellow slavery advocates were executed.

Southerners heard no preaching against slavery because they had purged the land of clergy who would deliver such messages: "In August 1859, two ministers of the Methodist Episcopal Church, Solomon McKinney and 'Parson' Blount were driven from Dallas by citizens of the city. McKinney was administered seventy lashes before his expulsion."[8] "A more serious consequence was administered to another 'Northern Methodist' minister, Anthony Bewley, who, during the night of September 13, 1860, was hanged by a Fort Worth vigilance committee that charged him with plotting a slave insurrection in Texas."[9]

Confederates defined the problem as agitation against slavery. Much of Southern honor society focused on speech. Violent response to offensive speech was condoned and encouraged. Abolitionist literature such as *Uncle Tom's Cabin* was banned throughout the South.

Southern post office employees confiscated abolitionist pamphlets and burned them.

SOUTHERN DUELING SOCIETY

Abolitionists argued that slavery desensitized Southern society as evidenced by the acceptance of dueling. Every time a duel was fought, there was a distinct possibility that at least one of the participants would die. Despite such serious consequences, Southern gentlemen felt compelled by their culture to defend their honor. The honor culture condoned and expected duels to be fought whenever one's reputation was slandered making duels a common practice.

The following murderous affray at Canton, Mississippi, is from the *Alabama Beacon*, Sept. 13. 1838.

'A terrible tragedy recently occurred at Canton, Miss., growing out of the late duel between Messrs. Dickins and Drane of that place. A Kentuckian happening to be in Canton, spoke of the duel, and charged Mr. Mitchell Calhoun, the second of Drane, with cowardice and unfairness. Mr. Calhoun called on the Kentuckian for an explanation, and the offensive charge was repeated. A challenge and fight with Bowie knives, toe to toe, were the consequences. Both parties were dreadfully and dangerously wounded, though neither was dead at the last advices. Mr. Calhoun is a brother to the Hon John Calhoun, member of Congress.

Here follows the account of the duel referred to above, between Messrs. Dickins and Drane.

Intelligence has been received in this town of a fatal duel that took place in Canton, Miss., on the 28th ult., between Rufus K. Dickins, and a Mr. Westley Drane. They fought with double barrelled guns. Loaded with buckshot—both were mortally wounded.[10]

The New Orleans correspondent of the *New York Express*, in his letter dated New Orleans, July 30, 1837, says:

THIRTEEN DUELS have been fought in and near the city during the week; five more were to take place this morning.'[11]

The widespread acceptance of dueling resulted in legalized murder. Survivors were not prosecuted. It was also difficult to convict those who murdered people in fights. Colonel John Wilson was president of the bank at Little Rock and Speaker of the House of Representatives of Arkansas. During a dispute, he murdered fellow representative Major Anthony with a large Bowie knife on the House floor. Despite all the members of the House witnessing the murder, Colonel Wilson was not arrested for a number of days. Wilson wined and dined the populace while awaiting trial. He dined with the jury during the trial. When found not guilty, there was widespread celebration. The murder of Major Anthony among many influential witnesses without a subsequent conviction illustrates reluctance of Southern justice to convict those who murdered while defending their honor.[12]

ARTICLES OF BATTLE BETWEEN JOHN A. WILLEY AND W. WHIPG HAZZARD.

Condition 1. The parties to fight on the same day, and at the same place, (St. Simon's beach, near the lighthouse,) where the meeting between T. F. Hazzard and J. A. Willey will take place.

Condition 2. The parties to fight with broadswords in the right hand, and a dirk in the left.

Condition 3. On the word "Charge," the parties to advance, and attack with the broad-sword, or close with the dirk.

Condition 4. THE HEAD OF THE VANQUISHED TO BE CUT OFF BY THE VICTOR, AND STUCK UPON A POLE ON THE FARM FIELD DAM, the original cause of dispute.

Condition 5. Neither party to object to each other's weapons; and if a sword breaks, the contest to continue with the dirk."[13]

Dueling was widely condoned and advocated by the upper class throughout the South. John Lyde Wilson, one-time governor of South Carolina, wrote a sixteen-page pamphlet, "Code of Honor," instructing participants on the etiquette of dueling. Louis T. Wigfall Senator from Texas fought a duel while in South Carolina in which both seconds went on to serve as governors of that state. His daughter records that he "was a firm believer in the Code duello as a factor in the improvement of both the morals and the manners of a community! He held that it engendered courtesy of speech and of demeanor—had a most restraining tendency on the errant fancy—and, as a preservative of the domestic relations, was without equal."[14]

The Southern concept of honor produced a difference between Southern and Northern societies that was noted by Ohio Congressman Giddings. In his journal entry for December 14, 1838 he wrote:

It is a fact, which every man of observation must see, by spending a few days in the Representatives' hall, that there is a vast difference in the character of the members from the North and South. . . [E]very person present must have witnessed the high and important bearing of the Southern men; their self-important airs, their overbearing manners, while the Northern men, even on the subject of slavery, are diffident and forbearing. I have myself come to the honest conclusion that our Northern friends are, in fact, afraid of these Southern bullies.[15]

Dueling was a natural extension of the jousts depicted in Romance literature. Risking one's life in duels demonstrated bravery which Southern culture equated with honor. If bravery equaled honor, the prevalence of duels would ensure a culture composed of honorable men, which would result in an honorable culture. With Southern men so concerned about their honor and willing to take extreme risks to defend it, one might expect such actions would produce an honorable society. Certainly, Southerners viewed themselves as living in such a culture.

SLAVE RIGHTS

Slavery raised the issue of the legality of murdering slaves throughout the South. Eventually, slave states decided that slave murder should be illegal. Slavery advocates pointed to such laws as evidence of the benevolent character of Southern slavery. Judge Clarke, of Mississippi, argued slave murder was illegal in the *State of Mississippi v. Jones*. He reasoned that some rights are more important than others, the most important being the right to life.

Because individuals may have been deprived of many of their rights by society, it does not follow that they have been deprived of all their rights.

... In this state the legislature have considered slaves as reasonable and accountable beings; and it would be a stigma upon the character of the State, and a reproach to the administration of justice, if the life of a slave could be taken with impunity, or if he could be murdered in cold blood, without subjecting the offender to the highest penalty known to the criminal jurisprudence of the country. Has the slave no rights, because he is deprived of his freedom? He is still a human being, and possesses all those rights of which he is not deprived by the positive provisions of the law.[16]

Judge Clarke's argument ran smack into the Declaration of Independence. The Declaration asserted that rights come from God, and governments are instituted to protect those rights. The Declaration proclaimed that the right of liberty came from God and Judge Clarke admitted that the state of Mississippi deprived slaves of that right. In his heart, Judge Clarke knew that slave murder should be illegal. To make this point, he admitted that slaves were people who had been deprived of the right of liberty by the government of Mississippi. It was impossible to reconcile this position with the Declaration.

Although Southerners admitted that slaves had a right to life, they refused to respect family relations. After John Brown's capture and trial, Maria Child accompanied the wife of John Brown as they visited him in prison before his execution. "Governor Wise mocked her feelings ... and then Senator Mason's wife chided all Northern women as hypocrites who did not know how to care for the unfortunate as well as the Southerners, who nurtured their slaves like family. . . Child memorably encapsulated the conflict of moral principles... of course free-state women performed all the charitable acts Mason had described with the exception that 'here at the North, after we have helped the mother we do not sell the babies.'"[17] The entire dialogue was published and distributed in 300,000 pamphlets.

REIGN OF TERROR

The Richmond *Daily Dispatch* reported that Brown's objective was to arm slaves with confiscated armaments who could then join him in fighting slaveholders.[18] Southerners were understandably frightened and distressed by this prospect. They judged the Northern response to the raid apathetic and Northerners unsympathetic toward Southern safety. Many Southerners suspected people from the North of being undercover abolitionists. Southern wrath made the South a dangerous place for Northerners to travel. William Lloyd Garrison published a 144 page pamphlet detailing vigilante atrocities perpetrated in response to Brown's raid titled *The New "Reign of Terror" in the Slaveholding States.*[19]

The objective of the pamphlet was to strengthen anti-slavery resolve. Many Northerners still sought to avoid conflict with the South out of respect for Southern white citizens. The pamphlet illustrated the degree to which slavery advocates demanded conformity with their beliefs in exchange for continued peace.

Garrison was not alone in reporting these events. "There exists at this moment, throughout the Southern States, an actual Reign of Terror. No Northern man, whatever may be his character, his opinions, or his life, but simply because he is a Northern man, can visit that region without the certainty of being subjected to a mean espionage over all his actions, and a rigid watchfulness over all his expressions of opinions; with the risk of personal indignity, and danger even to life and limb."[20] "Every day, fresh instances of banishment are occurring in all parts of the South. Northern men are coming away in armies—driven out of sixteen States, and made exiles in their own country."[21]

Garrison understood that the best way to persuade people was through the emotional impact of firsthand accounts. The pamphlet contained many such stories.

A book salesman visited an Alabama town selling *Fleetwood's Life of Christ,* published in the North. No one produced evidence of abolitionist activities by the salesman or abolitionist sentiments in the book. Nevertheless, because he was from the North selling a book published in the North, authorities decided he must be expelled. The case came before the Methodist Conference which shamelessly displayed their subservience to slavery dogma decreeing that such a book might endanger "Southern institutions."

The militia was assembled to escort the salesman out of town. A local music teacher who had migrated from the North nine years previously was summoned to play the flute at the head of the procession. This teacher had always spoken in favor of slavery but resented the injustice of the current exercise and declined participation.

This declination insulted Southern honor. That evening the music teacher received a letter threatening tar and feathers if he did not leave the state immediately. He saddled his horse at three A.M., leaving wife, family, and his business heading north.[22]

A Northern brick layer who scrupulously avoided commenting on slavery was employed in the South. One day an overseer decreed that a slave should receive 150 lashes for building an inadequate fire from green wood. Not wanting to get wet in the rain, the overseer administered the punishment inside. Wishing to avoid such a spectacle, the brick layer was drenched while waiting outside. Such silent censure offended Southern sensibilities. The next day, Southern gentlemen forced the brick layer to depart the South.[23]

Innocence provided ineffective protection. Frederic Schaller had lived in Missouri for twelve years. He never meddled in slavery and always supported the Democratic Party. Nevertheless, when slaves escaped, he was suspected. Three men placed him under house arrest. The following night, a mob took him into the woods and hanged him. He later described the brutality perpetrated upon him.

I caught the tree, but, by beating my hands with sticks, they compelled me to let go my hold. Soon I was senseless. When I came to again, I felt two persons, one on each side, whipping me with whips or cowhides. My hands were tied to the tree above my head, and I was entirely naked. The night was very cold, and soon my back was covered with a crust of frozen blood. I became weaker, and when they untied me, I fell to the ground. I heard one of them say, "Now you can go, you son of a bitch!" When I put on my clothes again, I found my money ($128 in gold) and watch gone. As I could not stand, I crawled, as well as possible, to a house of my father-in-law, where Dr. Niemeyer treated me.[24]

Seven people on the brig B. G. Chaloner , Capt. Kinney, his wife, Mr. Patterson the mate, and a crew of four, traveled south to pick up a load of lumber. When they went ashore, Southerners accosted them. Three crew members received 50 lashes, the last crew member received 100, Capt. Kinney and his mate received 54 lashes as Mrs. Kinney observed in horror. This atrocity was administered solely because the men were from the North.[25]

Garrison depicted the frenetic incidents as examples of Southern honor in action. He used the word "chivalry" to make his sardonic point. "…for it is a trait of Southern chivalry, first to practice cruelty, and then to suppress the facts."[26] "They were at once taken by the whiskey drinkers, stripped, threatened until they were terrified out of their wits, tarred and feathered, and ridden out of town on a rail! Such is Southern chivalry!"[27] "They seized him, and proceeded to beat him unmercifully. This assault was an outburst of chivalrous feeling. . . ."[28]

The concept of honor as embodied throughout the South tended toward anarchy. Acts which would ordinarily be unlawful were condoned whenever one's honor was offended. This situation was aggravated by the fact that the offense to one's honor was determined by the individual. Thus, many egregious acts were excused whenever the perpetrator felt his honor had been slighted. This situation intensified for Northerners throughout the South during the year between John Brown's raid and the outbreak of hostilities. They could expect to receive no protection of their rights whenever Southerners accused them of opposing the divine right of slavery.

In those days there was no king in Israel: every man did that which was right in his own eyes
(JUDGES 21:25).

CHAPTER SIX

SLAVE LIFE

And this is the condemnation, that light is come
into the world, and men loved darkness rather
than light, because their deeds were evil.

For every one that doeth evil hateth the light,
neither cometh to the light, lest his deeds
should be reproved.

But he that doeth truth cometh to the light,
that his deeds may be made manifest, that they
are wrought in God

(JOHN 3:19-21).

Southerners realized most abolitionists were
Northerners with no direct experience with slavery.
Under these circumstances, honor did not require
Confederates to divulge a candid assessment of their
peculiar institution. They could make up fictionalized
versions of slavery, in effect, challenging abolitionists to
prove them liars. As the slavery debate progressed in the
mid-1830s, Southern apologists like South Carolina
Congressman Waddy Thompson audaciously depicted

slavery as a blessing. "I regard African slavery, in all its bearings, as a blessing. . . . nowhere on the earth, in his native land or any other, is the African so elevated in the scale of being."[1]

Abolitionists who had spoken with runaway slaves knew this argument was preposterous. Theodore Weld and Angelina and Sarah Grimke set about collecting evidence to refute Southern narratives. They knew they could not raise Northern consciousness with a few anecdotes. Evidence would have to be extensive to be convincing. Personal accounts were difficult to obtain. Plantation owners normally did not discipline slaves in front of Northern audiences. Southerners who testified knew they could not return to the South without fearing for their lives. Nevertheless, calls went out for stories. They only published stories from reliable sources including Southern newspapers. They compiled 177 pages published in a book titled, *In American Slavery as it is: Testimony of a Thousand Witnesses.* It did not purport to present a balanced picture of slavery. It challenged claims that slavery as practiced in the South was a benign institution. This chapter contains a small selection of those accounts depicting a variety of horrors encountered by slaves.

Abolitionists acknowledged that there were slave owners who treated there slaves with more kindness than the stories depicted here. Harriet Beecher Stowe portrayed such in *Uncle Tom's Cabin.* All of us with some limb of our family tree containing a slave owner, have been assured that our ancestors treated their slaves kindly—more like pets really. Those with ancestral slave owners would include a majority of blacks judging from their lighter complexion in comparison to Africans. These vignettes question the morality of allowing a system to continue which could tolerate such gross abuses.

CHATTLE STATUS

Just as some ranchers preferred mixed breed cattle, some plantation owners preferred mulatto slaves. Some plantation owners bred their own slaves, but this led to complications. The wife's adamant objections diminished marital harmony. It also put owners in the awkward position of raising their own offspring as slaves. One plantation owner preferred instead to have a white acquaintance breed his slaves offering $20 for every slave he impregnated.[2] The owner treated his female slaves as livestock, illustrating the "elevated" level Africans experienced under Southern slavery.

RELIGIOUS INSTRUCTION

Since abolitionists argued against slavery on religious grounds, defending slavery required religious justification. Stories depicting Southern clergy as cruel and immoral were particularly effective in attacking their credibility by questioning their commitment to Christian principles.

I know a local Methodist minister, a man of talents, and popular as a preacher, who took his negro girl into his barn, in order to whip her—

and she was brought out a corpse! His friends seemed to think this of so little importance to his ministerial standing, that although I lived near him about three years, I do not recollect to have heard them apologize for the deed, though I recollect having heard ONE of his neighbors allege this fact as a reason why he did not wish to hear him preach.[3]

Moral instruction was provided by mothers as well as clergy.

A handsome mulatto woman, about 18 or 20 years of age, whose independent spirit could not brook the degradation of slavery, was in the habit of running away: for this offence she had been repeatedly sent by her master and mistress to be whipped by the keeper of the Charleston work-house. This had been done with such inhuman severity, as to lacerate her back in a most shocking manner; a finger could not be laid between the cuts. But the love of liberty was too strong to be annihilated by torture; and, as a last resort, she was whipped at several different times, and kept a close prisoner. A heavy iron collar, with three long prongs projecting from it, was placed round her neck, and a strong and sound front tooth was extracted, to serve as a mark to describe her, in case of escape. Her sufferings at this time were agonizing; she could lie in no position but on her back, which was sore from scourgings, as I can testify, from personal inspection, and her only place of rest was the floor, on a blanket. These outrages were committed in a family where the mistress daily read the scriptures, and assembled her children for family worship. She was accounted, and was really, so far as alms-giving was concerned, a charitable woman, and tender hearted to the poor; and yet this suffering slave, who was the seamstress of the family, was continually in her presence, sitting in her chamber to sew, or engaged in her other household work, with her lacerated and bleeding back, her mutilated mouth, and heavy iron collar, without, so far as appeared, exciting any feelings of compassion.[4]

This episode helps to explain the differences in religious concepts between the North and South.

CHILDREN
Children who were naturally repulsed at the sight of brutal punishment became hardened over time.

I had a class-mate at the Andover Theological Seminary, who spent a season at the south,—in Georgia, I think—who related the following fact in an address before the Seminary. It occasioned very deep sensation on the part of opponents. The gentleman was Mr. Julius C. Anthony, of Taunton, Mass. He graduated at the Seminary in 1835. I do not know where he is now settled.

I have no doubt of the fact as he was an eye-witness of it. The man with whom he resided had a very athletic slave—a valuable fellow—a blacksmith. On a certain day a small strap of leather was missing. The man's little son accused this slave of stealing it. He denied the charge, while the boy most confidently asserted it. The slave was brought out into the yard and bound—his hands below his knees, and a stick crossing his knees, so that he would lie upon either side in form of the letter S. One of the overseers laid on fifty lashes—he still denied the theft—was turned over and fifty more put on. Sometimes the master and sometimes the overseers whipping—as they relieved each other to take breath. Then he was for a time left to himself, and in the course of the day received FOUR HUNDRED LASHES—still denying the charge. Next morning Mr. Anthony walked out—the sun was just rising—he saw the man greatly enfeebled, leaning against a stump. It was time to go to work—he attempted to rise, but fell back-again attempted, and again fell back—still making the attempt, and still falling back, Mr. Anthony thought, nearly twenty times before he succeeded in standing—he then staggered off to his shop. In course of the morning Mr. A. went to the door and looked in. Two overseers were standing by. The slave was feverish and sick—his skin and mouth dry and parched. He was very thirsty. One of the overseers, while Mr. A. was looking at him, inquired of the other whether it were not best to give him a little water. 'No, damn him, he will do well enough,' was the reply from the other overseer. This was all the relief gained by the poor slave. A few days after, the slaveholder's son confessed that he stole the strap himself.[5]

HOMICIDE

Southerners pointed to laws prohibiting the murder of slaves as evidence of their benevolence. Although such laws did exist, they were not regularly enforced.

"One Mrs. Mann . . . was known to be very cruel to her slaves. She had a bench made purposely to whip them upon; and what she called her 'six pound paddle,' an instrument of prodigious torture, bored through with holes; this she would wield with both hands as she stood over her prostrate victim."

She thus punished a hired slave woman named Fanny, belonging to Mr. Charles Trabue, who lives near Palmyra, Marion co., Missouri; on the morning after the punishment Fanny was a corpse; she was silently and quickly buried, but rumor was not so easily stopped. Mr. Trabue heard of it, and commenced suit for his property. The murdered slave was disinterred, and an inquest held; her back was a mass of jellied muscle; and the coroner brought in a verdict of death by the 'six pound paddle.' Mrs. Mann fled for a few months, but returned again, and her friends found means to protract the suit.[6]

Among the servants waiting was a young negro man, whose beautiful person, obliging and assiduous temper, and his activity and grace in serving, made him a favorite with the company. The dinner lasted into the evening, and the wine passed freely about the table. At length, one of the gentlemen, who was pretty highly excited with wine, became unfortunately incensed, either at some trip of the young slave, in waiting, or at some other cause happening when the slave was within his reach. He seized the long-necked wine bottle, and struck the young man suddenly in the temple, and felled him dead upon the floor. The fall arrested, for a moment, the festivities of the table. 'Devilish unlucky,' exclaimed one. The gentleman is very unfortunate,' cried another. 'Really a loss,' said a third, &c. &c. The body was dragged from the dining hall, and the feast went on; and at the close, one of the gentlemen, and the very one, I believe, whose hand had done the homicide, shouted, in bacchanalian bravery, and southern generosity, amid the broken glasses and fragments of chairs, 'LANDLORD! PUT THE NIGGER INTO THE BILL!" This was that murdered young man's requiem and funeral service.[7]

A beloved friend in South Carolina, the wife of a slaveholder, with whom I often mingled my tears, when helpless and hopeless we deplored together the horrors of slavery, related to me some years since the following circumstance.

On the plantation adjoining her husband's, there was a slave of pre-eminent piety. His master was not a professor of religion, but the superior excellence of the disciple of Christ was not unmarked by him, and I believe he was so sensible of the good influence of his piety that he did not deprive him of the few religious privileges within his reach. A planter was one day dining with the owner of the slave, and in the course of conversation observed, that all profession of religion among slaves was mere hypocrisy. The other asserted a contrary opinion, adding, I have a slave who I believe would rather die than deny his Saviour. This was ridiculed, and the master urged to prove the assertion. He accordingly sent for this man of God, and peremptorily ordered him to deny his belief in the Lord Jesus Christ. The slave pleaded to be excused, constantly affirming that he would rather die than deny the Redeemer, whose blood was shed for him. His master, after vainly trying to induce obedience by threats, had him terribly whipped. The fortitude of the sufferer was not to be shaken; he nobly rejected the offer of exemption from further chastisement at the expense of destroying his soul, and this blessed martyr died in consequence of this severe infliction.[8]

The owner killed his slave, destroying his own property out of curiosity. He exhibited no fear of punishment despite laws prohibiting the murder of slaves.

Workload was not constant on plantations raising cotton and sugar cane. Plantation owners could not justify keeping a large workforce to cover peak periods. Therefore, they over-worked their slaves during the eight weeks of peak activity in which the slaves worked almost continuously. This practice led to an average life expectancy of only five years.[9] Owners made the decision based solely on economics that it was cheaper to buy replacement slaves than to maintain a larger number of slaves throughout the year.

HUMAN NATURE

God did not concentrate the morally challenged south of the Mason-Dixon Line. The reported abuses resulted from a culture that did not condemn and punish such conduct when directed toward slaves. "Human nature is no worse at the South than at the North; but law at the South distinctly provides for and protects the worst abuses to which that nature is liable."[10]

> From a knowledge of your own disposition and present feelings, your excellency will not be willing to believe that you could ever be brought to an act of tyranny, or even to execute justice with unnecessary rigor. But trust me, sir, there

is nothing more corrupting, nothing more destructive of the noblest and finest feelings of our nature than the exercise of unlimited power. The man, who in the beginning of such a career, might shudder at the idea of taking away the life of a fellow-being, might soon have his conscience so seared by the repetition of crime, that the agonies of his murdered victims might become music to his soul, and the drippings of the scaffold afford blood to swim in. History is full of such excesses.[11]

A judicious and benevolent friend lately told me the story of one of her relatives, who married a slave owner, and removed to his plantation. The lady in question was considered very amiable, and had a serene, affectionate expression of countenance. After several years residence among her slaves, she visited New England. 'Her history was written in her face,' said my friend; 'its expression had changed into that of a fiend. She brought but few slaves with her; and those few were of course compelled to perform additional labor. One faithful negro woman nursed the twins of her mistress, and did all the washing, ironing, and scouring. If, after a sleepless night with the restless babes, (driven from the bosom of their mother,) she performed her toilsome avocations with diminished activity, her mistress, with her own lady-like hands, applied the cowskin, and the neighborhood resounded with the cries of her victim. The instrument of punishment was actually kept hanging in the entry, to the no small disgust of her New England visitors.

'For my part,' continued my friend, 'I did not try to be polite to her; for I was not hypocrite enough to conceal my indignation.'[12]

"This man told me that he had rather whip a negro than sit down to the best dinner."[13]

The whole commerce between master and slave is a perpetual exercise of the most boisterous passions, and the most unremitting despotism on the one part, and degrading submissions on the other. Our children see this, and learn to imitate it. ... If a parent could find no motive either in his philanthropy or his self-love, for restraining the intemperance of passion towards his slave, it should always be a sufficient one that his child is present. But generally it is not sufficient. The parent storms, the child looks on, catches the lineaments of wrath, puts on the same airs in the circle of smaller slaves, gives loose to his worst of passions, and thus nursed, educated, and daily exercised in tyranny cannot but be stamped by it with odious peculiarities. The man must be a prodigy who can retain his manners and morals undepraved by such circumstances.[14]

Members of the planter class regularly observed cruelty directed toward slaves as they matured. Circumstances forced them to form moral opinions about these events. If they judged these events immoral and inconsistent with Christian principles, they would simultaneously be judging parents and family of gross hypocrisy and immoral depravity. Few could reach this conclusion.

Ultimately the question was one of rights and justice. Jefferson was intimately familiar with the injustices of slave life and the nature of unalienable rights. He argued that the slaves had a moral right to experience liberty. "But, as it is, we have the wolf by the ear, and we can neither hold him nor safely let him go. Justice is in one scale, and self-preservation in the other."[15]

CHAPTER SEVEN

SOUTHERN BELIEFS

He that turneth away his ear from hearing the law, even his prayer shall be abomination
(PROVERBS 28:9).

For the time will come when they will not endure sound doctrine; but after their own lusts shall they heap to themselves teachers, having itching ears;

And they shall turn away their ears from the truth, and shall be turned unto fables
(2 TIMOTHY 4:3–4).

EVOLVING MORALITY

Colonial churches believed and preached that slavery was a sin. Slave owners opposed this message most of whom were located in the South. Given the choice between owning slaves and receiving forgiveness for their sins through the shed blood of Jesus, most slave owners chose to retain their slaves.

Their descendants ratified this choice by continued defense of slavery. Missionary efforts in these instances resulted in few conversions causing clergy frustration and disappointment. Opposition to the slavery message curtailed most preaching opportunities and prevented all access to slaves.

Clergy disenchantment promoted compromise. Southern clergy agreed not to condemn slavery to gain access to slaves. As the abolition movement gained strength in its moral denunciation of slavery, Southerners looked to their clergy to refute abolitionist allegations. Clergy concessions over slavery progressed to publicly defending it before a candid world. After defending slavery for many years, clergy could not admit to their congregations or themselves that their position had been a compromise to gain access to slaves. They continued their pro-slavery rhetoric throughout the slavery debate in an effort to win a theological argument. By the time the Civil War began, Southern clergy were fully on record as defenders of slavery among family, friends, neighbors, Northern clergy, abolitionists, and informed citizenry worldwide.

Southern society inherited a legacy of deception from their forefathers. Over time, slave owners and advocates eradicated clergy who failed to pass slavery litmus tests. They threatened to tar and feather those who dared to return. Some they murdered. As such, Confederates bore responsibility for the moral teaching they received leaving them with priests who judged for reward, clergy who taught for hire, and prophets who divined for money. They loved to have it so.

Despite abolitionist tenacity in labeling slavery a sin, Southern clergy never hesitated nor faltered in persistently and passionately proclaiming the righteousness of the Confederate cause. It was a truth universally acknowledged in the seceding states that slavery was ordained by God and the Confederate cause was righteous. Most parishioners had heard nothing else. With the passage of time, Southern clergy had come to believe their carefully crafted defense of slavery while repudiating their church's initial convictions. Southern consensus fully expected God's support in their effort to secede.

SLAVE TRADE

The debate over the slave trade was an excellent illustration of how Southern clergy implemented this philosophy. Delegates to the Constitutional Convention recognized the inconsistency between the principles in the Declaration of Independence and slavery. They allowed for the continued importation of slaves prior to 1808 in Article I Section 9 of the Constitution implying that it could be terminated after that time. In 1808, Thomas Jefferson urged Congress to prohibit slave importation because it violated "human rights." The House of Representatives quickly passed the measure 113 to 5. Three senators voted against the law.[1]

As the slavery debate intensified in the 1850s, slavery advocates realized that the law against the importation of African slaves implied that slavery was immoral. A group of slavery advocates sought to rectify this logical inconsistency in their argument, agitating to make slave trading legal again.

The Methodist church had felt safe in preaching against the slave trade since it was the law of the land. The Nashville *Christian Advocate* referred to it as "supreme unrighteousness." However, facing censure from pro-trade advocates, the General Conference of the Methodist Episcopal Church, South, expunged a rule forbidding "The buying and selling of men, women and children, with the intention to enslave them," by a vote of 143 to 8. Faced with rabid pro-slavery, pro-trade rhetoric, church bishops perceived that "supreme unrighteousness" was actually "a purely civil institution."[2]

Unshackled by cleric moral pronouncements, politicians were free to debate the pros and cons of slave trade unhindered. To the chagrin of trade advocates, the Confederate Constitution contained an article forbidding the slave trade. "But, for God's sake, and the sake of consistency, do not let us form an union for the express purpose of maintaining and propagating African slavery, and then, as the Southern Congress has done, confess our error by enacting a constitutional provision abolishing the African slave trade."[3] Confederates had argued for secession to preserve racial management of slaves rather than from economics. They argued that emancipation would force them to socialize with ex-slaves on an equal basis, would endanger white women with rape from black men, and could result in a race war.[4] These arguments were necessary to convince subsistence farmers and lower class whites who owned no slaves and would bear the brunt of wartime casualties to support secession and the subsequent war. After making such claims, Confederates could not immediately instigate renewed slave trading.

CHURCH SCHISMS

Southern society was not the only source dictating the development of their cleric's theology. The environment included Northern abolitionists and clergymen. Because slavery was a moral issue debated in theological terms, the first schisms occurred in church denominations. While Southern clergy developed a politically acceptable doctrine, the more confrontational abolitionists enlisted support for their anti-slavery positions among Northern church members. As the slavery debate intensified in the 1830s, abolitionists argued that slaveholders were sinners and such sinners should not be allowed in churches nor should Christians fellowship with slaveholders who purported to be Christians. Church leadership in the North tried to remain neutral. Furious abolitionists argued that the church could not remain neutral on such a moral issue.

Southerners recruited their clergy to rebut abolitionist rhetoric in defense of slavery.

To the Editor of the Camden Journal:
The fanatics of the North oppose the institution of slavery, on the ground that it is immoral. They preach this from the pulpit—teach it in their schools, and inculcate it in every department of their social system. It strikes me that the clergy

of the South would render the most important service to their country by enforcing the opposite opinion that slavery is moral and well sustained by the laws of nature and the Holy Scriptures. It certainly is obligatory upon the clergy here to perform this duty with zeal, as their brethren in the North are so active against us.[5]

In response to the abolitionist assault on slavery, Southerners sought to force Presbyterians, Methodists, and Baptists to repudiate abolitionists.

The first schism over slavery occurred in the Presbyterian Church in 1837. The dispute included several issues. However, several synods had become predominately abolitionist. In 1837, the Old School or Reformed synods exscinded four New School synods which contained most of the abolitionists. Most of the Southern congregations remained with the Old School.

The first significant Methodist schism occurred in 1842 when a small group of anti-slavery congregations formed the Wesleyan Methodist Denomination. Three years later, Southerners forced the slavery issue with the appointment of slave-owning James O. Andrew as bishop. When the General Conference voted 110 to 63 to suspend Andrew, Southerners recognized this as condemnation of slavery. They voted to withdraw and formed the Methodist Episcopal Church South.

Baptist churches were relatively autonomous so that denomination had no general conference dictating a moral stance on slavery. However, Baptist churches supported the same missionary societies. In 1845, Alabama Baptists issued a hypothetical question to the boards governing these societies asking if they would appoint slaveholding missionaries. When the boards decided such an appointment would condone slavery, they replied they could not support such an appointment. Southern Baptists immediately seceded from these societies forming Southern equivalents.

For the most part, Northern denominations did not endorse harsh abolitionist policies maintaining a hope of reconciliation. This tepid response enraged strident abolitionists. Many within the churches agreed which initiated responses in each of the fragmented denominations.

The New School Presbyterians adopted harsher attitudes toward slaveholders causing the few remaining Southern churches in that assembly to split. Prior to this, the assembly called slavery a sin but did not judge the slaveholder considering him a victim of circumstances. In 1857, the assembly held the slaveholder responsible for slavery due to his engagement in slave activities.[6] Methodist who believed the immorality of slavery required a stronger response separated as Free Methodists in 1860 with a rule against fellowshipping with slaveholders. Baptist missionary and tract societies had refused to publish anti-slavery material. Northern Baptists who favored a stronger response formed separate missionary and tract societies to publish their views.

The depth of abolitionist resentment was manifested and illustrated at William Lloyd Garrison's funeral years after the war in 1879. The service was held in a church which had refused to allow abolitionist access for anti-slavery events. The speaker condemned the church for these actions in his Garrison eulogy: "The very pulpit where I stand saw this apostle of liberty and justice sore beset...yet it never gave him one word of approval or sympathy."[7]

Slavery advocates required total capitulation. When Northern churches refused to endorse the morality of slavery by appointing slave owners as missionaries and bishops, Southern churches split from Northern counterparts.[8] A parallel political tactic forced universal complicity in slavery through the *Fugitive Slave Act*, requiring everyone to participate in the apprehension and return of escaped slaves.

The apathetic policy of mainline denominations continued until the Civil War when reunification became impossible. At that point, church antislavery rhetoric became pointedly strident throughout the North. On December 23, 1860, three days after South Carolina seceded and before any other state seceded, Reverend Henry J. Van Dyke preached on the Character and Influence of Abolitionism. This sermon was answered by Reverend J. R. W. Sloane on January 9th. Both men were affiliated with the Reformed Presbyterian Church, which had expelled the synods with the most strident abolitionists. Sloane condemned slavery and Southern society which fostered it and, in the process, ridiculed its chief defenders, Southern clergy, to the fullest extent of his oratorical abilities. In so doing, he accused Southern clergy of serving Satan instead of God:

The Southern States of this Union are the great strongholds of Satan's kingdom, the seats of irreligion, impiety, and all wickedness have breathed the pestilential taste of that moral impurity all over the land, and have done and are doing a thousand-fold more against the cause of Christ than all the infidels that New England has ever produced. . . .

Make your home on the slopes of Vesuvius, and expect that it will not be rocked by the earthquake, or swept by the fiery flood, when it rolls from its burning crest; but do not expect that a nation can have peace which enslaves men, that a kingdom will stand which violates God's law; that a people can prosper who spoil the poor and oppress the stranger; that you can avert the wrath of Heaven with sermons against abolitionism, or turn back the arm of the Almighty when it is stretched out with prayers in which there is no confession of guilt, or promise of repentence toward God; or that your compromises and exhortations to peace will avail, when Jehova rides forth upon the whirlwinds when "the Lord thunders in the heavens, and the Highest gives his voice, hail stones and coal of fire."[9]

Once hostilities commenced, additional Northern clergy began to speak out against slavery. Church conventions began passing resolutions condemning slavery.[10] Reverend Garnet preached one of six fast day sermons condemning slavery summarized in *The Portage County Democrat*, Ravenna, Ohio, on May 13, 1863, blaming slaveholders for the war. Reverend Henry Beecher spoke in Manchester, England proclaiming that slavery was of the devil and that the South was fighting for an immoral cause.[11] As the war progressed, such sentiments were on the lips of many Northerners as they sang "The Battle Hymn of the Republic."

Southern papers occasionally reported on religious sentiment in the North to convince readers of Northern fanaticism:

RELIGIOUS FANATICISM IN THE NORTH.
The churches of the North are running stark mad with Abolitionism. Here are a series of resolutions passed by the "Synod of the Evangelical Lutheran Church" of Williamsburg, Pennsylvania, which, we are told, were adopted "without a dissenting voice."
Resolved, That, believing slavery to be the cause, animus and power of this rebellion, we regard the proclamation of freedom as the "axe laid at the root of the tree," and rejoice in it not only as a measure of war, but as an act of eternal justice which a Christian nation owes to the slave.[12]

Southern papers reported actions taken by the New York Methodist Episcopal Conference and the United Presbyterian Synod of Illinois condemning slavery: "…that slavery is incompatible with Christianity and republican institutions; that the conference concur in the righteousness of the President's proclamation of freedom to the blacks; …"[13] *"Resolved,* That the institution of slavery being at war with right; the interests of the nation, we regard it as the imperative duty of the executive to embrace the opportunities now afforded in Providence to secure liberty to all the inhabitants of the land."[14]

Northern arguments divided Confederate society into two groups: deceivers and deceived. The most influential deceivers were those in government, the press, and clergy. These groups felt it their duty to defend Southern honor.

DECEIVERS
Jefferson Davis's Proclamations
Confederate political leaders spoke often and passionately about their relationship to God and the righteousness of their cause. Jefferson Davis, President of the Confederacy, issued ten proclamations of humiliation, fasting, and prayer during the war. The first proclamation was issued on June 13, 1861, "Knowing that none but a just and righteous cause can gain the Divine favor . . . "[15] Davis's statement acknowledged that rational individuals could only expect Divine favor upon a righteous cause. Those who persisted in sin forfeited all expectation of God's blessing on their endeavors. Since Davis acknowledged the futility of praying for God's blessing upon an unrighteous cause, each succeeding proclamation implicitly bolstered the impression of Confederate righteousness.

The third proclamation was issued February 28, 1862[16]: "should pray that he may strengthen our confidence in his mighty power and righteous judgment.

Then may we surely trust in him that he will perform his promise and encompass us as with a shield." Davis was confused. God had promised the South nothing. We know this because the South lost the war. The war was fought over the promise made in the Declaration of Independence to God to create a government protecting everyone's inalienable right of liberty.

The eighth proclamation was issued April 8, 1864[17]: "...gratefully remembering the guidance, support, and deliverance granted to our patriotic fathers in the memorable war which resulted in the independence of the American colonies . . ." This proclamation referred to the favor granted to the colonies during the Revolutionary War. The Declaration of Independence sought God's favor during that war while promising to institute a government recognizing the inalienable right of liberty for everyone. Confederate leaders refused to accept responsibility for their debt to God to acknowledge and protect everyone's inalienable right to liberty while attempting to appropriate divine favor.

The final proclamation was issued March 10, 1865[18]: "that the Lord of Hosts ...will graciously take our cause into his own hand and mercifully establish for us a lasting, just, and honorable peace and independence." God could not take the Confederate cause into his hand because in was unrighteous. Ten fast days proclaimed under the mistaken conviction of Confederate righteousness failed to achieve the petitioned Confederate victory. However, God did grant a lasting, just, and honorable peace shortly after this proclamation.

Fasting and prayer were designed to assist in hearing God's voice and discerning his will. The South engaged in these activities to persuade God to favor their cause.

> **Wherefore have we fasted, say they, and thou seest not? wherefore have we afflicted our soul, and thou takest no knowledge? Behold, in the day of your fast ye find pleasure, and exact all your labours.**
>
> **Behold, ye fast for strife and debate, and to smite with the fist of wickedness: ye shall not fast as ye do this day, to make your voice to be heard on high.**
>
> **Is not this the fast that I have chosen? to loose the bands of wickedness, to undo the heavy burdens, and to let the oppressed go free, and that ye break every yoke**
> (ISAIAH 58:3, 4, 6)?

Journalistic Appeals

Journalistic appeals to Southern patriotism and sacrifice made ample allusions to God's favor and the righteousness of the Confederate cause. Although the writers were not professional proclaimers of righteousness, they consistently endorsed the justness of their cause.

If with so just and noble a cause, approved and assisted by the God of justice and truth, we fail from lack of courage, vigilance and enterprise, the failure will cover us with eternal shame and contempt. The fact, then, that God is with us, that He inspires and directs our deliberations, plans and fights our battles, controls all our affairs in the council chamber and on the field of battle, and strengthens and sustains the hearts of the people—that precious fact should make us more faithful in the performance of our duties, and more careful to abstain from every evil.

If the light of God's countenance shines upon our cause, that cause has claims upon us that we dare not turn our backs upon. The voice of Government is the voice of God, and all its requirements and commands are clothed with authority and power. It simply gives utterance to obligations which have been binding by the Lord of all, and in making known these duties, the Government we ourselves created simply acts as the organ and instrument of the King of Kings and Lord of Lords.

This consideration vastly augments the force of the obligations made incumbent by citizenship. And in refusing to meet them, in refusing to comply with the demands of patriotism, we violate the commands of Heaven, and are doubly criminal in the sight of God.[19]

Southern apologists argued that "the voice of Government is the voice of God." In fact, this article implies that if Southerners reached a different conclusion than the government, they would "violate the commands of Heaven."

Southern Clergy

Clergy communicated their beliefs in the righteousness of the Confederate cause in numerous ways. Governing bodies of denominations published resolutions and Christian journals published articles asserting their beliefs. Speeches, prayers, and sermons were published. The mode of communication did not alter the message. Southern clergy were united behind the Confederate cause, convincing Southern soldiers that God was on their side and would assure them ultimate victory. "When the Civil War had become an actuality, Southern Methodists were almost wholly on the side of the Confederacy."[20] Methodist Bishop Andrew in a letter printed in the *Southern Christian Advocate* in June, 1861 said, "He believed that the South would be victorious because their purpose was righteous. . . Finally, he asserted that many Southern soldiers were earnest Christians, as were the people at home, and the united prayers of all the people in behalf of their cause would certainly prevail."[21]

Resolutions

Reverend Mr. Hilliard, Rector of the Chapel of the Cross, Chapel Hill authored the resolution for the Episcopal Church of North Carolina.

Resolved, That in this day of our national trial, the Protestant Episcopal Church in North Carolina, confident in the justice of the cause for which the people of the Confederate States are contending . . .

Resolved, That, believing that righteousness alone, in the end, either exalteth or saveth a nation, she pledges herself to put forth all her energies for the cultivation, by God's help, in the Southern people, of those virtues which win the favor, and for the eradication of those vices which cannot but incur the wrath, of the King of Kings and the Lord of Lords.

Resolved, That her fervent prayers shall ever ascend to her Heavenly Master, that He will endow our rulers with wisdom, and crown our arms with victory.[22]

The phrase, "Heavenly Master," implies a willingness to do whatever God requires. When the colonies pledged to form a government guaranteeing everyone's right to liberty, the nation was obligated to honor that pledge. The concept of honor is not limited to complying with the requirements of pledges to other people. We must also comply with pledges made to God. Reverend Hilliard and the Episcopal Church felt they could win God's favor, convincing him to support the Confederate cause by cultivating virtues and eradicating vices, but they would not consider complying with their pledge by eradicating slavery.

The Holston conference issued a resolution supporting one of President Davis' fast days.

> the only alternative left them in the Providence of God, is to appeal to the Sovereign of the Universe for the righteousness of the cause, and under His blessing and guidance, to organize for themselves a Government founded upon the great principles of justice and equity, for mutual protection and for the better security of all those rights of religion and good society guaranteed to us and all other peoples by the God of heaven. It can not now be gainsaied with all the lights before us, that to the people of the Confederate States has been committed, in a sense true of no other people on the face of the globe, the guardianship and moral and intellectual culture of the African race, and that the Methodist Episcopal Church South is, to a great extent, charged, in the providence of God, with the religious destiny of the colored man.[23]

In a failed attempt to justify past compromises and support of slavery, the Methodist Church proclaimed itself guardian of the "moral and intellectual culture" and "religious destiny" of the black race. Is that really the way God wanted them to reach the black race? If Methodists truly believed that God guaranteed "all those rights of religion and good society . . . to us and all other peoples," they could not support slavery.

The Baptists in South Carolina concurred in the justness of the Confederate cause. "Resolved. That the results of the past two years have only confirmed the conviction expressed by this convention at its last session, that the war which has been forced upon us, is, on our part, just and necessary...."[24] "The President laid before Congress a communication from the Chowan Baptist Association, of South Carolina, accompanied by a series of resolutions expressive of confidence in the Government of the Southern Confederacy, and the justness of the southern cause."[25]

Christian Journal
Reverend Dr. Palmer of New Orleans defended South Carolina against charges that secession resulted from chronic hatred of the national union.

> relying on nothing save the righteousness of her cause and the power of God, she took upon her shield and spear as desperate and as sacred a conflict as ever made a State immortal. It is just this heroic devotion to principle, this faith in the right and the true, this singleness of heart in the presence of duty, and this abiding trust in the power and righteousness of God, that render her capable of a thousand martyrdoms, and incapable of political bondage.[26]

Speeches
Reverend Regester displayed Southern learning, et cetera. in his speech to the citizens of Staunton, Virginia.

We have not heard the address, but have been informed by those whose pleasure it has been to hear it, that it fully sustains the reputation of the Rev'd gentleman for learning, research and eloquence. The object of the address is to present the religious and moral aspect of this all absorbing question, and to show that it demands our fullest belief in its righteousness and in our ultimate success.[27]

Reverend Dr. Palmer welcomed Confederate soldiers to entertainment provided by the Ladies of Columbia. After reiterating the righteousness of their cause, the Reverend Doctor reminded his listeners that they were fighting for freedom.

many a heart accustomed to hold communion with Heaven has invoked the watchful providence of Almighty God to throw around you the shield of protection... with their hearts solemnly impressed with the fear of God, were not afraid to pit their State against all the fortunes of this fearful and bloody war. ... All alone, but upon a platform as high as our own Blue Ridge, a spectacle to the world, and immediately under the eye of the Great God of Hosts and God of Battles, we are fighting for the right and for the true. ... with a religious trust in the power of Almighty God, we of the South, in our infancy, all alone, will grapple with our foes until God, in his own time, shall grant us our freedom . . .[28]

West Point graduate Leonidas Polk became a bishop in the Protestant Episcopal Church of the Diocese of Louisiana. As the war began he was appointed a General of Division No. 2, located at Memphis, Tennessee. In a pastoral letter, he informed clergy and laity that Episcopalians also believed in the justness of the Southern cause. "Of the justice of our cause we have no doubt. . . . We have taken our stand, we humbly trust, in the fear of God, ..."[29]

Prayers

Bishop Atkinson of the Episcopal Church issued a prayer to be used by the churches in his diocese in observance of President Davis' fast day on May 16, 1862.

O, most Glorious and Gracious Lord God, the Lord of Hosts, mighty in power, and of majesty incomprehensible; who art a strong tower of defence to all who flee to Thee for succor, we, Thy suppliant people, now beseech Thee to save and deliver our afflicted country in this her day of sorrow and trial. Rebuke the pride and malice of her enemies. Give, in increasing measure, Righteousness and Wisdom to our Rulers; strength and success to our Armies; Faith and Fortitude, and devout obedience to all our people. Restore to us speedily, O God, the blessings of Peace, and make it appear that Thou art our Saviour and mighty Deliverer, through Jesus Christ our Lord. Amen.[30]

Bishop Atkinson instructed Diocese members to pray for a Confederate victory to prove that God had been on their side. This thought coupled with defeat would later challenge Southern faith.

Bishop Green of Mississippi expressed his conviction in the righteousness of the Confederate cause in a prayer for Southern armies.

> Watch over our fathers, and husbands, and brothers, and sons, who, trusting in Thy defence and in the righteousness of our cause, have gone forth to the service of their country. ... so overrule events and so dispose the hearts of all engaged in this painful struggle, that it may soon end in peace and brotherly love, and lead not only to the safety, honor and welfare of our Confederate States, but to the good of Thy people and the glory of Thy great name . . .[31]

In an attempt to convince God to favor the Confederate cause, Green told God that Confederate victory would bring glory to his name.

Southern Christians attempted to invoke John 14:13, 14 in an effort to require God to ensure Confederate victory.

> PRAYER FOR THE COUNTRY.—The usual prayer meeting for the country will be held at Wesley chapel, at 4 ½ o'clock, on Monday evening next. The present crisis is fraught with momentous interest to the people

of the Confederate States. The Ruler of the universe hath declared that whosoever shall ask anything of Him, nothing doubting, the same shall be granted. If we truly desire peace and independence, all we have to do is with humble faith to beseech the Omnipotent God to crown our arms with success in the battles now progressing in Virginia, and pending in North Georgia. We trust that every lover of his country will attend the prayer meeting at Wesley chapel on Monday next.[32]

Skeptical Christians would question Confederate application of this promise. If Northern Christians applied the same verse, how would God answer both prayers? The answer lies in the definition of the word, "ask." In the Greek this word carries with it the implication of "demanding what is due." In other words, before applying this verse, Christians must first determine what is due. In this case, the founding document of the nation had pledged a different outcome.

Sermons

Southern clergy were not reticent or hesitant in preaching Confederate righteousness from pulpits. "you are engaged in a cause sacred by every tie of humanity and self-preservation, to remember that under the protection of the Ruler of the Universe, you cannot but successfully carry forward the cause in which you have embarked."[33] "God controls the destinies of the battle field, and makes triumphant those that contend for the right."[34]

Reverend Wilson passionately preached Southern arguments in a lengthy sermon.

> We are engaged in a great work, it is the cause of independence and the maintenance of our just rights. . . . Our cause is just and right; an inherent right to freedom, independence, and self-government; and we are certain of success if we will be governed by the proper spirit.

> . . . remonstrating again and again, against a legislation unjust, unconstitutional, and at war with our civil, religious, and political institutions, and destructive to the peace and prosperity of our country . . . .[35]

Listening to the reverend, one would assume the Confederate Constitution contained some newly found rights not protected in the US Constitution, rights which Northerners and current citizens do not enjoy. This was not the case. If the reverend had been truthful with his congregation, he would have admitted that they were fighting for only one thing, the right to own slaves, something that the Republican platform of 1860 already granted them. Wilson's argument would have been more convincing if he had named the unjust legislation. If he had done so, we could examine that legislation to determine if his accusations were true.

Reverend Wilson talked about understanding the will of God. "Our duties and obligations so far as we have been able to understand, the will of the Divine mind is not submission."[36] Southern clergy were unable to determine the will of God from the brutality of slavery. They were unable to determine the will of God from the pledge in the Declaration of Independence. Despite Reverend Wilson's assurances that being in God's will would ensure Confederate victory, Southern clergy were unable to determine the will of God even after the Confederate defeat. What we have here is a widespread, determined, and concerted resolve to misinterpret the will of God.

Reverend Wilson expanded his defense of Southern righteousness.

It is surely time for us to be freed from such an eternal intermeddling with privileges secured to us both by the laws of God and man. . . . Our cause, I verily believe, is the cause of God. . . . It is a combat for principle, against envy, pride, ambition, and fanaticism; a contest for civil and religious liberty, against an absolute and oppressive despotism; a contest for the strict observance of solemn pledges, and a wilful determination to sacrifice the solemn and sacred obligations of good faith; and last, but by no means least, it is a contest for the true interpretation of the sacred Scriptures, against false construction and infidel assumptions of the Divine writings.[37]

If Reverend Wilson had been truly convinced of the righteousness of the South's cause, he would have freely admitted they were fighting to continue Negro slavery. Wilson referred to "privileges secured to us both by the laws of God and man." Since Confederates were fighting to preserve slavery, he was saying owning slaves was a privilege given to Southerners by God. Reverend Wilson referenced solemn pledges without naming any, yet he and his congregation habitually chose to ignore the pledge made by the colonies to grant everyone equal rights to life, liberty, and the pursuit of happiness in the nation's founding document.

Confederate Chaplains

Of all Confederate deceivers, chaplains had the most blood on their hands. They were the most invested in the righteousness of the Confederate cause. Wartime enlistees knew they put their lives in peril. In such a time, some found Walter Scott's honor morality insufficient. They sought assurance that death did not end in oblivion. Confederate chaplains were the ones who convinced soldiers of the righteousness of their cause as they entered battle. They were the ones who had listened to confessions from dying soldiers voicing their faith that they would receive divine approval as they reached Heaven's gates.

Confederate chaplains had to protect soldiers from Northern rhetoric proclaiming slavery immoral. Reverend J. C. Granberry described wartime preaching: "It was always assumed that the cause for which they contended was righteous; on it was invoked the divine blessing, and the troops were exhorted to faithful service."[38]

Chaplains believed and preached that God's favor depended on eradicating sin and faith-filled prayer. In a speech, Reverend Ryland identifies greed and drunkenness as the besetting sins denying God's blessings to the Confederacy.

> Greed and avarice have taken possession of the hearts of many, while in every portion of the confederacy distilleries have been springing up, ... It is the decree of the heaven that 'righteousness exalteth a nation, but sin is a reproach to any people.' It is vain to speak of the justice of our cause, unless we seek upon that cause the blessing of heaven . . . .[39]

By identifying greed and drunkenness as the major obstacles to obtaining divine favor, Ryland implied that Southerners need not concern themselves about the morality of slavery. Slavery was not included in the South's approved list of sins for clergy.

Uniformity of belief provided chaplains confidence in seeking full support from Confederate churches. Reverend Lacy composed a letter seeking such support while serving on a committee with Reverend Jones who published it in a book more than twenty years later. Lacy expressed the view that the Confederate cause must be righteous because it was supported by the government: "Is the Church as much alive to its duty as the State? Duties never conflict. Our patriotism will be all the stronger and purer when sanctified by religion. … To patriotism must be added the mightier principle of faith. Let love of country be joined to love of God. …"40

Scripture never instructs the church to receive guidance from government. Nevertheless, the paper written by chaplains and newspaper articles attest that this was a common concept in Confederate society. Chaplains expected little to no argument from the recipients of their paper. The accolades accorded the chaplains' paper by Reverend Jones in his book revealed that this concept remained after the war. In other words, the Confederate cause was not righteous because God declared it so but because government declared it so. Those unskilled in biblical exegesis could confidently rely upon the legality of any issue to determine its morality.

Lacy's argument was inconsistent. These same Christians had been citizens of the United States just two short years earlier. Why did his principles not apply to that government? The war was fought over two opposing government principles. The Northern principle said that slavery should not extend into the territories. The Southern principle said that slavery must be defended and that Northern citizens should support it. Both government principles could not be sanctioned by God. Lacy proposed a principle that could not withstand logical scrutiny and Jones continued to laud it years later.

Lacy correctly identified the crux of the chaplain's dilemma: "the Church, to the full extent of its ability and opportunity, is responsible for the souls of those who fall in this conflict."[41] Unfortunately for Lacy, it was possible for duties to conflict. Lacy had to decide whether his loyalties lay with God or the Confederate Army. Lacy chose the army. He exercised his responsibility by convincing soldiers their cause was righteous before sending them into battle to defend slavery. Obviously, Lacy saw no inconsistency between legalized slavery and Christian virtues, but there were Christians in the North who disagreed.

Lacy called upon the South to "prostrate itself at the foot of the Cross": "If ever a nation was called to prostrate itself at the foot of the Cross, and to suplicate the mercy of God with strong crying and tears, it is this. God, we believe, will deliver us from our enemies, but that deliverance must come in answer to prayer."[42] That was good advice, but there is no evidence that Lacy ever stopped to consider what it meant. It is a way of life in which Christians submit their wills to Jesus. Unfortunately, Lacy did not know the will of Jesus. The pressing physical needs of the army drowned out the Lord's voice as well as logic applied to scripture. Lacy was unaware that the army was fighting against the Lord because he had hardened his heart to what the Lord was saying about slavery.

Lacy joined Southern clergy in preparing for the eventuality of Confederate defeat: "If the want of faithfulness on the part of the Church, the impiety of the army and the people, should prevent God's blessing, then the unfaithfulness of the Church will have blasted our hopes, destroyed our country, and left a continent in ruins."[43] Lacy was convinced the church would be guilty if the Confederacy suffered defeat. When the war was lost, Lacy's words placed responsibility on the church, but the church refused to accept it. The want of faithfulness and prayer were not mentioned as possible causes of defeat.

Lacy acknowledged that defense of Confederate righteousness required a truthful argument: "A higher estimate has been placed upon *truth* and upon *right* by a people resisting unto blood, striving against sin. We may indulge the hope that the results which God designed are following from the war."[44] Lacy vastly overstated the South's search for truth. Southerners censored abolition literature. Thomas Jefferson had argued for freedom of speech by pointing to the hope that truth could defeat lies. If Southerners were concerned with truth, they would have responded to abolitionist arguments rather than censoring them.

Lacy expressed hope that the result God designed would follow from the war. The significant results from the war were the preservation of the union and freedom for slaves. After the war, pride in Southern hearts would not allow them to accept that God designed these results. Unfortunately, going without food for a day did not eradicate pride.

DECEIVED

The success of the Confederate campaign to convince Southern citizenry concerning the righteousness of their cause is illustrated in their writings.

The Bird Family

The Bird family had many connections through kinfolk to influential and wealthy Southern clans. They owned the Granite Farm plantation in Hancock County, Georgia where two-thirds of the inhabitants were slaves. Their plantation was near Sherman's march but escaped damage. An overseer assisted Sally in managing the plantation while Edgeworth served in the Confederate Army. Two generations of the family owned 45 slaves.

The Bird family was convinced that the South's cause was righteous: "With a firm reliance upon God, who will ever be on the side of right, I am willing to cast myself into the gap and dare to 'Nobly stem tryannic pride or nobly die a second glorious part that my country may be free.'"[45] Sally Bird seems to imply that God was obligated to answer their prayers, and they could pray any desired outcome into existence: "Thank God for our victories out West and one in N.C.—in Va.—in Fla.—everywhere so far—and may the God of Battles be our aid in the great contests about to come on. I feel, indeed, that all of us ought to be on our knees."[46]

As evil tidings continued to pour in from the war front, the Birds continued to look to God for deliverance and ultimate victory. "I'll hope and trust in our good God. My faith never waivers that all will be right."[47] "All will yet be well . . . . God will yet bless our cause."[48] "Our affairs do wear rather a gloomy look just now, but, by God's blessing, I hope better times are ahead."[49] "I have this item in my creed, that God will arrange us all for our good, if we act our parts according to our most sincere convictions of right."[50] The barrage of gloomy war reports must have affected Sally Bird's faith by this time. She did not express confidence in the righteousness of the Confederate cause but on the South's "sincere convictions of right." However, God dispenses divine favor on the cause which is actually righteous, not the cause with the most deceived adherents.

Belle Edmondson

As a woman, Belle Edmondson could not join soldiers in battle but served instead as Confederate spy and courier. "We all attended prayer meeting, and observed our President's fast day."[51] "Vicksburg, surrendered this morning and an exulting foe, madened by success, imagines the Rebellion crushed—poor deluded fools—tis just begun. Tis God's will you should prosper, and devastate our lovely land so far . . . yet our faith is perfect. God will bless us. . . . We are content my Savior, thy will, not ours, be done. 'Blessed is the man, whose trust is in thee.' God is our Sun and Shield, and we will yet come out victoriously free."[52] Edmondson thought her faith was perfect, but faith must be based upon the will of God. Faith that opposes God's will can never be perfect.

Edmondson, along with her Southern compatriots, continued to denounce the Northern cause as sinful. She could not bring herself to consider the possibility that the South was defending an evil institution in violation of the nation's covenant with God. "Our Armys all seem to be Status Quo. God grant successful may be the termination of 1864. Oh! My savior I have buried the past. Guide and leade me from temptation. After you my God, then I live for my Country. God bless our leaders in Dixie."[53] "Merciful Father crown our Armys with Victory. Spare so much bloodshed of the bravest and best of our Sunny South. Enlighten the minds of the miserable Yankees, of their sinfulness. Drive them from our soils! Oh, just and merciful Saviour, give us peace, and our independence."[54]

Edmondson attempted to convince God to grant the South victory by reminding him of war casualties. "Oh! my heavenly Father … think of the thousands of Souls hastened into eternity… ."[55] "Give us peace then will we praise thy great and glorious reign through all eternity."[56] Edmondson promised to praise God if he gave the South peace, but what good are her promises after the South reneged on the promise to grant and protect everyone's right to liberty?

Mary Boykin Chesnut

Mary Chesnut was married to James Chesnut. They lived on Mulberry Plantation outside Camden, South Carolina. James Chesnut served as United States Senator for two years prior to the war. He served as aide to Jefferson Davis and was promoted to Brigadier General toward the end of the war. Mary Chesnut does not reveal her own beliefs concerning the righteousness of the Confederate cause, but she does reveal the prevailing sentiment. "These women have all a satisfying faith. 'God is on our side,' they cry. When we are shut in, we, Mrs. Wigfall and I, ask: 'Why?' Answer: 'Of course, He hates the Yankees!"[57] "At dinner, Mr. Hunter said: 'The parsons tell us every Sunday that the Lord is on our side. I wish, however, he would show his preference for us a little more plainly than he has been doing lately.'[58] General Chesnut expressed the following sentiments in a letter to Mary Chesnut transcribed in her diary for February 26, 1864. "I trust still in the good cause of my country and the justice and mercy of God."[59]

OBITUARIES

Southern obituaries consistently expressed confidence in the righteousness of the Confederate cause, "a gallant and true soldier in the noblest cause of justice and right ever committed to human hands. . . ."[60] "and gave his life to her holy cause."[61] "…it is a consolation to your parent and friends to know that you died in a glorious cause…"[62]

TESTIMONIALS

Enlistees in the Confederate Army, steeped in Southern beliefs, had no consciousness of opposing God's will. There were numerous stories of Confederates testifying of their faith as they lay dying. Christians expressed confidence in their rapid ascension to Heaven as they trusted that the death of Jesus paid for their sins.[63]

Unidentified soldier: "Captain, I am going to die … tell them I die in a good cause—fighting for my country, and in Christian faith."[64]

Unidentified soldier: "while dying he felt he had tried to discharge his duties both as a soldier and Christian."[65]

Unidentified soldier: "'Mother, here is the Bible you gave me—I made good use of it.' He died in triumph, exclaiming, 'Not my will, but thine, O God, be done.'"[66]

Unidentified soldier: "May heaven grant that if I fall a martyr in the cause of my country, my kindred and their posterity may be proud that they had a relative who offered his life upon the altar of liberty."[67]

Testimony of a fellow officer concerning Major John Stewart Walker: "It is impossible to separate his character as a soldier and as a Christian. He was a soldier because he was a Christian; and while he fought manfully against the enemies of his country, his fervent spirit labored and fought earnestly against the enemies of his Lord."[68]

Lieutenant Mangum: "he only bewailed the conviction that, falling in the first conflict, he had done so little for a cause that he honestly esteemed worthy of the sacrifice of life itself."[69]

The concept of martyrdom's glory and eternal rewards was reinforced throughout Southern society. "A correspondent of the Religious Herald writes: 'Not long since it was my privilege to standby the bedside of one of the heroes who are daily offering themselves as sacrifices upon the altar of their country.'"[70]

GOD'S WILL

The actions of Christians in the Confederate Army evidenced a conviction that Jesus created the black race for perpetual, generational slavery and their fight to defend that institution was righteous. Not one ear ever heard a discouraging word when the righteousness creed was proclaimed. Since obedience is a major part of the Christian life, it should not be difficult to determine God's will.

The Southern defeat contradicted the Southern belief system. It required a new explanation of Southern society and its relationship to God. Perhaps God was a fable. Perhaps he was distracted. Perhaps he did not intervene in the affairs of men. Perhaps God did not approve of slavery and could not support Confederate efforts to maintain it. Few were willing to accept the last explanation.

CHAPTER EIGHT

CRISIS OF CONSCIENCE

For the leaders of this people cause them to err;
and they that are led of them are destroyed
(ISAIAH 9:16).

WARTIME CAUSE

Even as the Civil War began, Confederates faced a crisis of conscience. They believed they were a righteous people fighting for a righteous cause. In their hearts, all knew they fought to preserve slavery.

Grant and Malinda Taylor were subsistence farmers in west central Alabama. When the Confederacy instituted a draft of able-bodied men from eighteen through thirty-five in April of 1862, Grant, at thirty-four, volunteered to serve in the 40th Alabama Infantry. He served as a private for the remainder of the war. With no slaves, Malinda ran the farm and raise their four children. The Taylors were forced to sell their farm and move into town before war's end.

The Confederacy was in a desperate situation as the year 1865 began. The shortage of soldiers caused some Confederate leaders to consider arming slaves in the fight to preserve the institution of slavery. Taylor expressed the camp consensus on this proposal in a letter to Malinda.

> General Baker and other officers are in favor of putting negroes into our brigade as soldiers. ... They are to be set free if they fight well at the end of the war if we gain our independence. ... The men, I believe, are generally opposed to it and a great many declare they will go home if they are put in ranks with us. That is my notion. And then to think we have been fighting four years to prevent the slaves from being freed, now to turn round and free them to enable us to carry on the war. The thing is outrageous.[1]

Southern antebellum society valued and protected honor as it related to reputation and that attitude continued as the war commenced. This caused Southerners to oppose any facts that implied Southern society was immoral. Southerners knew that most nations opposed their view and defense of slavery.

> on the 20th of May, 1861, the gallant freemen of the whole State will throw off the galling yoke of tyranny imposed by the miserable descendants of Puritanism. We now virtually stand alone in the eyes of the scrutinizing world, appealing to the rectitude of our intentions, the justice of our

cause, and the God of Battles to shield us from the poisoned darts of a calumnious foe.[2]

To avoid universal condemnation, Southerners quickly sought a cause separate from slavery. During the war, they proclaimed their cause to be freedom and liberty.

Everyone, including soldiers, readily accepted and rapidly became proficient in expressing their politically acceptable rationale for the war:

> But most Southern volunteers believed they were fighting for liberty as well as slavery. 'Our cause,' wrote one in words repeated almost verbatim by many, 'is the sacred one of Liberty, and God is on our side.' A farmer who enlisted in the 26th Tennessee insisted that 'life liberty and property [i.e., slaves] are at stake' and therefore 'any man in the South would rather die battling for civil and political liberty, than submit to the base usurpations of a northern tyrant.' ... A wealthy planter who married one of Mary Todd Lincoln's sisters became an officer in the 4th Alabama to fight for 'Liberty and Independence.' 'What would we be,' he asked his wife, 'without our liberty? ... [We] would prefer Death a thousand times to recognizing once a Black Republican ruler ... altho' he is my brother in law.'[3]

They saw no reason why the Revolutionary War cause would lose its righteousness.

Confederate obituaries cleansed slavery from the narrative leaving only the cause of freedom and liberty. "He fought gallantly, and died fearlessly. Thus do they all fall, brave and noble boys; their heart's best blood is lavishly poured out, as a sacrificial offering for the freedom of their country..."[4] "and caused his life's blood to be poured forth as a libation upon the altar of liberty."[5]

The Confederate Congress repeatedly referred to this cause in an 1864 address.

> Quite recently, scores of regiments have re-enlisted for the war, testifying their determination to fight until their liberties are achieved. . . . Their services above price, the only remuneration they have sought is the protection of their altars, firesides and liberty. ... We seek to preserve civil freedom, honor, equality, firesides; and blood is well shed, when 'shed for our family, for our friends, for our kind, for our country, for our God.' . . . we can, with the blessing of God, avert the perils which environ us, and achieve for ourselves and children peace and freedom.[6]

Jefferson Davis stated this objective in his proclamation for the South to humble itself in prayer on May 16, 1862. "We struggle to preserve our birthright of constitutional freedom."[7]

The Confederate argument was incomplete without enumerating the abuses and usurpations Northern aggression forced upon them and the relief they anticipated. Confederate apologists failed to provide such examples. The Confederate congress acknowledged that their government was modeled after the Constitution of the United States.

> As in the English Revolution of 1688, and ours of 1776, there was no material alteration in the laws beyond what was necessary to redress the abuses that provoked the struggle. … We have had our Governors, General Assemblies and Courts; the same electors, the same corporation, 'the same rules for property, the same subordinations, the same order in the law and in the magistracy.'[8]

Southern secession would have achieved no increase in liberties apart from greater protection for slavery.

Wartime rhetoric portrayed Confederates as noble people willing to make great sacrifices for freedom and liberty. However, their inability to identify specific freedoms these sacrifices would achieve while simultaneously denying basic, fundamental freedoms to slaves required suspension of logic exposing them to widespread, indefensible ridicule. The irony of men fighting to defend their right to own slaves while proclaiming it liberty obliged Lincoln to comment in a speech worth quoting at length.

> The world has never had a good definition of the word liberty, and the American people, just now, are much in want of one. We all declare for liberty; but in using the same word we do

not all mean the same thing. With some the word liberty may mean for each man to do as he pleases with himself, and the product of his labor; while with others the same word may mean for some men to do as they please with other men, and the product of other men's labor. Here are two, not only different, but incompatable things, called by the same name—liberty. And it follows that each of the things is, by the respective parties, called by two different and incompatable names—liberty and tyranny.

The shepherd drives the wolf from the sheep's throat, for which the sheep thanks the shepherd as a liberator, while the wolf denounces him for the same act as the destroyer of liberty, especially as the sheep was a black one. Plainly the sheep and the wolf are not agreed upon a definition of the word liberty; and precisely the same difference prevails today among us human creatures, even in the North, and all professing to love liberty. Hence we behold the processes by which thousands are daily passing from under the yoke of bondage, hailed by some as the advance of liberty, and bewailed by others as the destruction of all liberty. Recently, as it seems, the people of Maryland have been doing something to define liberty; and thanks to them that, in what they have done, the wolf's dictionary, has been repudiated.[9]

Lincoln's speech demonstrated how widely Confederate histrionics expressing their love of freedom was acknowledged throughout the North. Lincoln's audience required no further background information.

Lincoln's mild, humorous rebuke of the blatant contradiction in the Confederate argument would surely have been followed by more pointed ridicule and derision if Confederates persisted in this argument. Their argument required them to explain how liberty and freedom could be so vital to them while simultaneously being inconsequential to slaves. Proclaiming such hypocrisy before a candid world required a level of hubris unachieved by even the most rabid Confederates.

However, Confederates had a more fundamental reason for abandoning the "freedom and liberty" rationale for seceding after defeat. During the war, Confederates linked victory with freedom and defeat with slavery.

> Superadded to these, sinking us into a lower abyss of degradation, we would be made the slaves of our slaves, hewers of wood and drawers of water for those upon whom God has stamped indelibly the marks of inferiority. . . . We may find in all this an earnest of what, with determined and resolute exertion, we can do to avert subjugation and slavery . . . . Others look with alarm on the complete subversion of constitutional freedom by Abraham Lincoln and feel in their own persons the bitterness of the slavery which three years of war have failed to inflict on the South.[10]

If Southerners persisted in their argument, defeat would imply they lost their freedom and became slaves. Southern honor could accept no such conclusion. Finding themselves unprepared to declare themselves slaves, logic and dispassionate reflection forced postbellum apologists to abandon the cause they had asserted during the war.

Before the war, it was universally acknowledged that the North and South argued over slavery. As battle deaths grew, Confederates found that cause distasteful. They decided they were fighting for freedom and liberty. After the war, Confederates settled on states' rights as their cause demonstrating ubiquitous befuddlement. Based upon the historical record, a gullible observer could draw no other conclusion than that Confederates only figured out why they seceded after the war.

WHAT WENT WRONG

Confederate defeat deepened the Southern crisis of conscience. The Civil War pitted two Christian opponents with opposite views on the morality of slavery. In such a situation, the outcome of the war would of necessity have moral implications.

Convinced of their own righteousness, Confederates had capitalized on Southern victories to mock Northern moral condemnation of slavery.

RESPONSE TO LINCOLN'S FAST.

The good Book says the prayers of the wicked are an abomination, etc., and the Savannah

Republican thinks it has never been more strikingly illustrated than by recent events. Lincoln ordered a forward movement in Virginia, and simultaneously, but to proceed, a day of national humiliation, fasting and prayer. The papers inform us that the religious appointment was religiously observed, especially in the Abolition capitol. The armies of the North then moved forward, and we have Heaven's response in the late glorious victory for the Confederate arms.

It follows, that Lincoln must be brought to doubt either the efficiency of prayer or the righteousness of his cause. We should take it that he is staggered, for the more he prays and "pegs away," the worse he is whipped.[11]

By pointing out that the forces of the "abolition capitol" lost the battle, the writer implied that God endorsed slavery. Confederates found such ridicule humorous at the time. However, those whose conscience demanded consistent theology would find this argument convicting after the war.

Northern bards were not silent in this battle of dueling virtues. Parson Brownlow was a Methodist minister before he wrote editorials for a Whig newspaper and became active in politics. Although he supported slavery, he opposed secession. He sarcastically pointed out that Confederate prayers did not guarantee victory either.

This, Mr. Editor, is the never-to-be forgotten 18th of September, 1862, the day set apart by Jeff. Davis' proclamation as a day of humiliation and prayer and thanksgiving to God, for the favor he showed the rebels in front of Richmond and Washington in days gone by! It occurs to me that they ought to appoint another day for prayer, and take back all their expressions of gratitude for the manner in which providence has allowed them to be treated by "the Northern hordes" on the borders of Maryland and Pennsylvania! They should now marshal all their hypocritical preachers and old whisky-drinking clerical rips, and, with a united voice, heaving and setting at a throne of grace, like so many old rams at a gate-post, pray to their deity to save them from their friends, whilst they take care of their enemies![12]

It mattered not how clever the retort or exuberant the praise. The bards' frenzied proclamations produced no victories. Orators conceded that the final verdict would be delivered by God on the battlefields. They confidently left the decision in his hands.

Theologians had biblical justification for believing God would intervene on the side of the righteous.

Behold, the righteous shall be recompensed in the earth: much more the wicked and the sinner
(PROVERBS 11:31).

Unfortunately for Confederates, their theological position coupled with the war's outcome led to an unacceptable conclusion. Nevertheless, Confederate society refused to connect military defeat with a rhetorical rout.

Reverend Stephen Elliott, rector of Christ Church in Savannah, expressed the truth to motivate his congregation after the defeats of Gettysburg and Vicksburg. "We have assumed a very grand but a very solemn position, and we cannot, without utter shame and confusion of face, abandon it, and confess that we have been trusting in vain and unfounded expectations."[13] Clergy could not utter this truth once final defeat transformed it from possibility to fact.

If Southern logic was correct during the war, it had to be correct after the war as well. If the war was a judgment for the sin of slavery, then God ensured the ultimate Union victory. Southerners were correct in assuming many Northerners would draw this obvious conclusion.

While northern Methodists proclaimed that the Civil War was being waged to preserve the Union, they also declared that the contest was God's chastisement visited upon the nation for permitting the evil of slavery to exist for almost a century after the Declaration of Independence had been issued."[14] "The course of the war was considered as conclusive proof that God had somehow led and guided the North and confounded the South.[15]

Confederate clergy and civil leaders encouraged their populace in the war effort, preaching on and trusting in two fundamental principles: 1) The Confederate cause was righteous, and 2) because the Confederate cause was righteous, God would ensure their victory: "Our cause is just and right; an inherent right to freedom, independence, and self-government; and we are certain of success if we will be governed by the proper spirit."[16] Southern defeat proved beyond a doubt that at least one of these principles was false. Those who rejected the first principle were forced to admit that slavery was immoral, and its defense resulted in disastrous consequences. Confederates refused to accept this hypothesis. Instead, they began developing a narrative designed to defend their honor. The purpose of this invention was to defend the righteousness of the Confederate cause which, by implication, would simultaneously prove the second principle false. In effect, they argued God let down righteous Confederates who had trusted in him.[17] This narrative quickly became known as the "Lost Cause."

MORAL DILEMMA

The need for an alternative narrative for many had spiritual origins. Slavery had been debated over moral issues. Abolitionists stridently argued that slave owners outrageously denied God-endowed rights to slaves implying that all who supported slavery were morally depraved. However, Christians throughout the South remained unconvinced, ardently seeking God's help.

The obvious contradiction between Confederate beliefs and ultimate defeat caused a crisis of faith among honest Christians.[18] Ella Gertrude Clanton Thomas questioned her beliefs.

Slavery was done away with and my faith in God's Holy Book was terribly shaken. For a time I doubted God. The truth of revelations, all—everything—I no longer took interest in the service of the church...Our cause was lost. Good men had had faith in that cause. Earnest prayers had ascended from honest hearts—Was so much faith to be lost? I was bewildered—I felt all this and could not see God's hand.[19]

Clergy could confess to Christians like Ella Thomas that they made a mistake about the righteousness of slavery and the Confederate cause or support Lost Cause contentions. Confession might be good for the soul but can be devastating for the ego. God's spokespersons were having none of it. Their emotionally self-motivated investigation eventually perceived anointing on Lost Cause arguments while thundering against materialism and drunkenness which had never been taught and argued as God-ordained conditions.

Moses Drury Hoge pastored a Presbyterian church in Richmond during the war. As a volunteer chaplain, he preached regularly at a training camp. He ran the Northern blockade traveling to England to obtain over 300,000 Christian items to distribute to Confederate troops. After the war, he suffered from depression for a year before convincing himself that the South's cause had been righteous.[20]

Confronting universal confusion of face, Southern clergy advocated continued resistance when Southern society was conceding defeat. Reverend Hoge proposed a day of humiliation, fasting and prayer. The Confederate Congress authorized such an observance settling on Friday, March 10, 1865. It was the last such day observed by the South. The wording proposed by Hoge was not used, but his proposal prepared for Jefferson Davis's signature accurately reflected his beliefs.

Hoge repeated part of Jefferson Davis's argument from his eighth proclamation recalling the divine favor experienced by colonialists during the Revolutionary War. "recognizing the providence of God in the affairs of men, and gratefully remembering the guidance, support and deliverance granted to our patriot fathers in the memorable war which resulted in the independence of the colonies in the days of the first revolution."[21] Both Hoge and Davis believed the South's and the colonies' moral conditions were similar. The colonies were fighting for freedom as was the South. Slavery was legal in the colonies as it was in the South. Hoge viewed the favor God granted the colonies as evidence of divine intervention in affairs of state and approval of societies condoning slavery. God does not change. Hoge could see no reason God would withhold the same favor toward the South. However, the situations were different in one very important respect: The colonies pledged to form a government recognizing the truth that God had endowed everyone with an equal right to liberty. Abolitionists argued throughout the slaver debate that the South chose to ignore that principle. Hoge evidenced no comprehension of its significance.

Hoge believed the South was fighting for civil and religious freedom "the present struggle for civil and religious freedom . . ."[22] This belief required practiced self-delusion since the South was, in fact, fighting to deny civil and religious freedom to slaves.

Hoge's proposal repeated the Davis exhortations to Southerners to repent of sins so God could grant them victory. "penitently confessing their sins, ... [that God would] so manifest Himself in the greatness of His goodness and the majesty of His power, that we may be safely and successfully led through the trials of this just and necessary war,"[23] Confederate clergy were willing to repent of any sin but slavery.

Hoge expressed his anguish over the Confederate defeat in a letter to his sister.

I forget my humiliation for a while in sleep, but the memory of every bereavement comes back heavily, like a sullen sea surge, on awaking, flooding and submerging my soul with anguish. The idolized expectation of a separate nationality, of a social life and literature and civilization of our own, together with a gospel guarded against the contamination of New England infidelity, all this has perished, and I feel like a shipwrecked mariner thrown up like a seaweed on a desert shore.

I hope my grief is manly. I have no disposition to indulge in querulous complaints. God's dark providence enwraps me like a pall; I cannot comprehend, but I will not charge him foolishly; I cannot explain, but I will not murmur.

To me it seems that our overthrow is the worst thing that could have happened for the South— worst thing that could have happened for the North, and for the cause of constitutional freedom and of religion on this continent.[24]

Southern clergy used biblical arguments to counter abolitionist charges. Hoge worried that the war's outcome supported abolitionist exegesis.

Zillah Brandon

Zillah Brandon expressed confusion and anger over her situation at the war's conclusion.

Though now crushed by overwhelming numbers, despoiled of every right claimed by a free people, oppressed, driven by a storm that caused our country to founder. Yet our enemies cannot rob us of our birthright Truth and Honor. While we feel that we have been conquered by might rather than right, we are not degraded. The grand patriotism of '76 is burning in our souls as brightly as if it had been of this hours kindling.[25]

Brandon must have been unaware of Southern attacks on the Declaration of Independence as she lauded the patriotism of '76. Southern patriotism toward the Union had always been conditioned on acceptance of slavery.

Governor McDuffie provided an example of "Confederate truth" in the slavery debate. "Whether we consult the sacred Scriptures, or the lights of nature and reason, we shall find these truths to the effect that slavery is the status most conducive to the happiness of the African race as abundantly apparent, as if written with a sunbeam in the heavens."[26] This statement offends common sense. If it were true, we would see blacks today seeking masters. Since this is not the case, we know the statement is blatantly false similar to many other statements made by pro-slavery advocates. Brandon failed to acknowledge these brazen fabrications while naively hoping the God of truth would expend more effort defending her cause. Her claim to a birthright of "Truth and Honor" was a fantasy based on rationalization.

Abolitionists had regularly proclaimed the self-evident truths of the Declaration of Independence in their fight against slavery. The Declaration truths agree with Scripture's depiction of God as a father without favorites. They argued that a gracious God created everyone with equal rights, implying that whoever denied people these rights were opposing God's plan and purpose. They were, therefore, intentionally or unwittingly fighting against God. In response, Governor McDuffie expounded Southern "truths." Southern truths proclaimed that God created a favored race destined to rule an inferior race, demonstrating profound puzzlement and confusion.

Brandon felt the Confederates were despoiled of every right claimed by a free people. This statement manifested obvious indifference about the rights of slaves. Southerners had despoiled every right claimed by slaves without any sense of shame, and Brandon was unable to acknowledge that truth. Brandon expressed relief that the South's "enemies cannot rob us of our birthright Truth and Honor." That was true. Southerners were the only ones who could strip Southerners of truth and honor which they did by not honoring the Declaration pledge included in the country's founding document recognizing that God had endowed the right of liberty to blacks as well as whites.

Brandon felt that as long as Confederates believed the South was "conquered by might rather than right" they were not degraded. She expressed the overwhelming necessity for Southerners to believe this story. It made no difference whether or not this were true, as long as they believed it, they could avoid shame.

J. William Jones, Confederate chaplain and author of *Christ in the Camp*, expressed his dismay and ambivalence at the moral implications of Confederate defeat while his belief in the righteousness of the Confederate cause remained unshaken. "Lord we acknowledge Thee as the all-wise author of every good and perfect gift. . . . But we believe Thou will admit the grave mistake in giving the decision to the wrong side in eighteen hundred and sixty-five."[27] His statement highlighted the implication of the Southern defense of their righteousness. If Southerners were righteous, then God made a mistake. They could only hope God would be more diligent in determining their eternal abode.

Despite the universal ignorance of their covenant, many Confederate soldiers became Christians during the war. Speaking on the desire of Confederate soldiers to hear the gospel, Reverend Jones spoke of,

[The] great revival along the Rapidan in August, 1863, which reached nearly the whole army, and really did not cease until the surrender at Appomattox."[28] "The great revival which swept through our camps on the return of the army from the Gettysburg campaign, and which resulted in the professed conversion of thousands and the quickened zeal of Christians generally, naturally produced a desire to have houses of worship during the winter."[29] "There were forty chapels built along the Rapidan in the winter of 1863-1864, and over sixty the next winter along the Richmond and Petersburg lines."[30]

Reporting on the situation in the spring of 1864, Reverend William Bennett reported that the revival was increasing. "The awakening has been very extensive. Strong men bow themselves, and the man hardened by three years of war and the corrupting influences of the camps comes to the altar of prayer and 'mourns his follies past,' praying God for pardon."[31] No one knows how many conversions resulted from a conviction of personal sinfulness and the need of a savior and how many resulted from the erroneous idea that God could be enticed to fight for the South if enough soldiers became Christians. Conversions had no noticeable impact on the conviction that slavery was sinful among new converts. Confederates could have been tempted to interpret the revival in the Southern army as evidence of divine favor on their cause. However, Jesus came to seek and save sinners, and all who were fighting against his will certainly qualified.

Federalism

Just as conditions forced Confederates to abandon the cause of freedom following defeat, circumstances required hasty philosophical retreats in other proposed arguments. Edward A. Pollard envisioned the dishonorable heritage Southerners would leave their progeny if they did not act immediately to control the narrative. His book, *The Lost Cause, A New Southern History of the War of the Confederates*, published the year after Appomattox, sought to limit the damage to Southern honor.

Pollard began his book with an attack on Federalism.[32] He insinuated that the war was inevitable due to the Federal system of dividing power. Therefore, the war could not have been caused by a dispute over slavery. This principle is not included among current "Lost Cause" assertions since the Federal system has worked well, and there is no consensus that the system is abusive enough to warrant revolution.

Morality of Slavery

Another Pollard tactic was to decree that the slavery debate had not been waged over moral issues. "The slavery question is not to be taken as an independent controversy in American politics. It was not a moral dispute."[33] "We shall not enter upon the discussion of the moral question of slavery. ... For, we repeat, the slavery question was not a moral one in the North, unless, perhaps, with a few thousand persons of disordered conscience."[34] This obvious attempt to avoid moral responsibility revealed an underlying religious motivation for this part of Pollard's argument. It attempted to answer the charge that the Confederate defeat resulted from Divine judgment which could only result from a moral issue. Pollard evaded justifying these assertions by providing an alternative rationale for the abolitionists' arguments. If the debate was not waged over moral issues, why did abolitionists oppose slavery? Abolitionists did not oppose slavery on economic grounds.

However, the subject Pollard raised is central to an understanding of the Civil War and subsequent development of the "Lost Cause" myth. Noted historian Arthur M. Schlesinger concluded that a moral judgment concerning slavery was necessary for accurate understanding of the Civil War. "A society closed in the defense of evil institutions thus creates moral differences far too profound to be solved by compromise. Such a society forces upon every one, both those living at the time and those writing about it later, the necessity for a moral judgment; and the moral judgment in such cases becomes an indispensable factor in the historical understanding."[35] Those who wish to fully comprehend the issues leading up to the Civil War and its aftermath must engage in the moral debate. They must decide whether or not slavery was moral and study the time period based upon their conclusion.

Abolitionists used every means and argument available to convince fellow citizens about the immorality of slavery. Slavery was a moral issue to Congressman Feny.

> For six years have the supporters of Mr. Lincoln been striving to secure those Territories from the pernicious influences of the system of bondage. . . . they have been doing this because they thought that the extension of slavery by the national authority would bring down the vengeance of Heaven upon a guilty land.[36]

Sarah Grimke, abolitionist and co-author of *American Slavery as it is: Testimony of a Thousand Witnesses,* boldly stated her moral understanding of slavery.

> This blessed war is working out the salvation of the Anglo-Saxon as well as of the African race. The war is the holiest ever waged, is emphatically God's war, and whether the nation will or not, He will carry it on to its grand consummation, until every American enjoys the rights claimed for them in our Declaration of Independence.[37]

Frederick Douglass criticized most churches for not living by Christian principles on the slavery issue.

They strip the love of God of its beauty, and leave the throne of religion a huge, horrible, repulsive form. It is a religion for oppressors, tyrants, man-stealers, and thugs. It is not that *"pure and undefiled religion"* which is from above, and which is *"first pure, then peaceable, easy to be entreated, full of mercy and good fruits, and without partiality, and without hypocrisy."* But a religion which favors the rich against the poor; which exalts the proud above the humble; which divides mankind into two classes, tyrants and slaves; which says to the man in chains, *stay there*; and to the oppressor, *oppress on*; it is a religion which may be professed and enjoyed by all the robbers and enslavers of mankind; it makes God a respecter of persons, denies the fatherhood of the race, and tramples in the dust the great truth of the brotherhood of man.[38]

In plotting out his abolition strategy, William Lloyd Garrison concluded that the abolition of slavery had to become a moral endeavor before it could become a political one.[39] John Brown "liked to say that he believed in only two things, the Bible and the Declaration of Independence...."[40]

Perhaps the most effective abolitionist literature was *Uncle Tom's Cabin*. It appealed to the moral sensibilities of readers by portraying the evils of slavery. Through her character, St. Clare, Harriet Beecher Stowe speaks with unconstrained clarity and prophetic insight.

on this abstract question of slavery there can, as
I think, be but one opinion. Planters, who have
money to make by it,--clergymen, who have
planters to please,--politicians, who want to rule
by it,--may warp and bend language and ethics
to a degree that shall astonish the world at their
ingenuity; they can press nature and the Bible,
and nobody knows what else, into the service;
but, after all neither they nor the world believe
in it one particle the more. It comes from the
devil, that's the short of it;--and, to my mind, it's
a pretty respectable specimen of what he can do
in his own line.[41]

Stowe names those she holds most responsible for the
continuation of slavery; planters, clergy, and politicians,
charging that they were of the devil's line.

Slavery was a moral issue for abolitionists and was,
therefore, a moral issue for all who were influenced
by their arguments. Daniel Webster was not an
abolitionist. He was a politician who considered the
greatest national threat to be the agitation of the slavery
issue. Nevertheless abolitionist opposition to his policies
made him realize that the subject of slavery, "has not
only attracted attention as a question of politics, but it
has struck a far deeper-toned chord. It has arrested the
religious feeling of the country; it has taken strong hold
on the consciences of men."[42]

Slavery was a moral issue for everyone who felt
that slavery was immoral. Abolitionists throughout

the world argued against slavery on moral grounds. Pollard's failed attempt to argue otherwise illustrated the crisis of conscience that overcame Southerners after defeat. Assurances from clergy as well as the rest of society concerning the righteousness of their cause and the inevitability of a successful conclusion to the war had proven false. Confederates desperately sought some means to evade the moral implications of defeat.

Pollard's assertion was never fully accepted or supported by "Lost Cause" apologists. After near universal assurances by Southern clergy, many Southerners who had experienced and observed the abuses of slavery still questioned its morality and were unwilling to admit they fought a war to preserve it. Pollard's early efforts to evade moral indictments failed common sense tests. Nevertheless, "Lost Cause" apologists continued developing a more nuanced narrative that could survive casual scrutiny.

Southern clergy faced the possibility that at least some of their congregants would feel betrayed. Would Southerners hold clergy responsible for deceiving blind fools who had bravely hazarded life and limb opposing God's will? Would Southerners admit they had been gullible buffoons duped into believing an obvious lie? Southern clergy had anticipated this possibility. They warned congregants that God might not support their cause if they treated slaves inhumanely.[43] However, after the war, clergy opted for the "Lost Cause" explanation. In a vain attempt to salvage their honor, they failed to confess their moral blindness. Southern bravery on the battlefield did not extend to moral bravery after the war. Instead, Southerners conjured up and supported a fable depicting the South's experience as a righteous, heroically defended "Lost Cause."

CHAPTER NINE

CONFEDERATE'S LOST CAUSE

**He that covereth his sins shall not prosper: but
whoso confesseth and forsaketh them shall have
mercy**
(PROVERBS 28:13).

The primary message of the Lost Cause narrative is
that God did not intervene in the Civil War. Since
God is not capricious, this argument implied that
God does not judge nations these days. This hypothesis
must by necessity also include the idea that God does
not reward righteousness in this life for Confederates
trumpeted and continue to maintain that their cause
was righteous.

The religious environment motivating the Lost
Cause was composed of several aspects. Southern
clergy had defended slavery for decades in debates with
abolitionists and Northern clergy. Family, friends, and
neighbors had heard Southern clergy exegesis on favored
slavery texts. The objective of false starts, inconsistencies,
and eventual propositions was to obscure the condition
of hearts in a society desperately seeking to escape the
moral and religious consequences of slavery. Charles

Wilson in *Baptized in Blood* emphasized that Southern clergy, and in particular Confederate chaplains, led the proliferation and defense of the Lost Cause myth.[1]

Abolitionists did not debate Lost Cause apologists, not wanting to present obstacles to Southern repentance. Nevertheless, most Southerners could not consider repentance which would require admitting their error and accepting responsibility. The implications of the abolitionist position were so loathsome to Southern thinking that it could not be thought, let alone uttered. It would mean that Southerners were not righteous or virtuous; that their efforts to preserve the enslavement of black men were devoid of honor. Southern arrogance and stubbornness would have added the deaths of 620,000 soldiers, the maiming of many more, and destruction of the Southern economy to the moral sin of enslaving blacks for hundreds of years. They could imagine their grotesque souls fully exposed before a candid world.[2]

Such was the situation Southerners faced as they considered bequeathing a notorious legacy to their heirs. Concern for their reputation prevented them from acknowledging the truth. They opted instead to develop a narrative grounded in obfuscation. This narrative included a number of assertions, which became known collectively as the Lost Cause.

1 The Confederacy was defeated militarily only because of the Union's overwhelming advantages in men and resources.

2 The Civil War was fought over states' rights, not slavery.
3 African Americans were "faithful slaves," loyal to their masters and the Confederate cause and unprepared for the responsibilities of freedom.
4 Secession was legal.
5 Confederate soldiers were heroic and saintly.
6 The most heroic and saintly of all Confederates, perhaps of all Americans, was Robert E. Lee.
7 Southern women were loyal to the Confederate cause and sanctified by the sacrifice of their loved ones.

Any discussion of the basis for the Lost Cause explanation of the Civil War must include a discussion of the veracity of Lost Cause tenets. This assumes that it is possible to discern the truth, that we are not trapped in an intellectual morass void of moral and factual absolutes. It assumes Southern leaders were capable and motivated to express the provocations which forced secession.

Although the argument that slavery was not a moral issue is not explicitly included in the Lost Cause propositions, that thesis is the core motivation for the myth and is subtly implied in remaining contentions. One way the Lost Cause implied that slavery was not a moral issue was by eliminating God from the debate. Confederates began to eliminate mention of God from their Civil War narrative within hours of Lee's surrender at Appomattox.

ELIMINATING GOD

Reason for Defeat

Robert E. Lee demonstrated his Christian faith throughout the Civil War, encouraging conversions and Christian conduct by soldiers in the Army of Northern Virginia. Immediately after defeat at Gettysburg, Lee displayed his faith, seeking divine intervention on behalf of the South's "just cause" by endorsing Jefferson Davis' proclamation for a day of fasting, humiliation, and prayer:

Proclamation from General Lee

"HEADQUARTERS, ARMY NORTHERN VIRGINIA,
"AUGUST 13, 1863.

The President of the Confederate States has, in the name of the people, appointed August 21st as a day of fasting, humiliation, and prayer. . . . Soldiers! We have sinned against Almighty God. We have forgotten His signal mercies, and have cultivated a revengeful, haughty, and boastful spirit. We have not remembered that the defenders of a just cause should be pure in His eyes; that 'our times are in His hands,' and we have relied too much on our own arms for the achievement of our independence. God is our only refuge and our strength. Let us humble ourselves before Him. Let us confess our many sins, and beseech Him to give us a higher courage, a purer patriotism, and more determined will; that He will convert the hearts of our enemies; that He will hasten the time when war, with its sorrows and sufferings shall cease, and that He will give us a name and place among the nations of the earth.

"R. E. LEE, GENERAL."[3]

Lee referenced the clerical litany of safe preaching sins. He attributed to God the power to grant victory to his army if everyone repented.

To maintain the credibility of a just "Lost Cause," Confederates shunned all further mention of God intervening in the war after Lee's surrender. A different explanation of the Confederate defeat was required. Lee himself was the first to avoid mentioning divine intervention while rationalizing Southern defeat. Robert E. Lee's General Order Number 9 written to the Army of Virginia attributes the Southern defeat to only one source, "overwhelming numbers and resources."

General Order
No 9
After four years of arduous service marked by unsurpassed courage and fortitude, the Army of Northern Virginia has been compelled to yield to overwhelming numbers and resources. ...[4]

This immediately became the official Lost Cause rationalization for the Confederate defeat. "Ex-Confederates attributed their ultimate defeat solely to the overwhelming force of the Federal armies. Henry L. Wilson stated that 'we were overpowered and forced to surrender,' and added that 'genius and valor went down before brute force.'"[5]

WHAT'S ALL THE FIGHTING ABOUT?

As Southerners sought to eliminate God from the historical understanding, they simultaneously sought to claim for themselves a just and righteous cause which could only be based on standards established by the Deity. The title of the Confederate myth implies that Southerners had a psychological need to view themselves as defenders of a just cause. Such a cause deserved and demanded universal proclamation. Many obituaries had described their subjects as fighting for liberty and freedom. This would have been an acceptable cause if Confederates had won the war. Defeat made it unpalatable, requiring Confederates to find a cause they would not mind losing. Eventually, apologists settled on "states' rights" despite the absence of obituaries lauding fallen heroes for defending this cause. This is the key premise upon which the Lost Cause myth is based. This is the cause the South admits to losing in the Civil War. If this premise fails, the entire myth falls.

The major argument employed to defend the "just cause" proposition, as it related to slavery, was to deny that the South fought to preserve it. Before the war, Confederates warned the North that they would secede if the North failed to silence abolitionists. The disputes over slavery leading up to the Civil War were well known: the Missouri compromise, the Wilmot Proviso, the compromise of 1850 ("I have, Senators, believed from the first that the agitation of the subject of slavery would, if not prevented by some timely and effective measure, end in disunion."[6]), bleeding Kansas, dispute over the *Fugitive Slave Act*, church splits, the gag rule in Congress, Lincoln/Douglas debates, et cetera. The only comparable dispute over states' rights was the nullification dispute in 1831 which had been resolved many years before the Civil War.

Everyone agrees, including Southern historians, that a Southern victory in the Civil War would have resulted in the continuation of slavery. "Your conclusions about slavery are not a sure thing. I think it entirely dependent on the results of the rebellion. If we come out with flying colours, it is established for centuries."[7] Despite this, preachers of Lost Cause mythology insist that the South fought the Civil War to promote states' rights. This is probably the most widespread case of selective amnesia in the history of mankind.

The effect of this disinformation persists. Unbiased historians having studied antebellum heated arguments defending slavery and the South's rhetoric through the war conclude that the South seceded to protect and continue that institution. Most historians agree that precepts included in the myth of the Lost Cause have been discredited including the view that the South fought for states' rights.[8] Yet, this realization has not filtered down to the public whose opinions continue to be influenced by Lost Cause apologists. The Pew Research Center interviewed 1,507 people by telephone from March 30 to April 3, 2011, asking their impression of the main cause of the Civil War. Only 38 percent thought it was about slavery, while 48 percent thought it was about states' rights, and 9 percent answered both equally.[9]

Attempts by Southern writers to concoct an alternative cause for the Civil War were tacit admission that they lost the slavery debate. Several factors contributed significantly to the outbreak of hostilities, but eventually they all came back to slavery as Lincoln stated in his Second Inaugural Address. "One-eighth of the whole population were colored slaves, not distributed generally over the Union, but localized in the southern part of it. These slaves constituted a peculiar and powerful interest. All knew that this interest was somehow the cause of the war."

Secession Commissioners

Charles B. Dew, author of *Apostles of Disunion*, grew up steeped in Lost Cause mythology. He was convinced that anyone who did not believe the South fought the Civil War to preserve states' rights was either "deranged or a Yankee, and neither class deserved to be taken seriously."[10] At that point, his underdeveloped curiosity failed to wonder what specific rights his ancestors fought to gain.

As a college history professor, Dew discovered letters and speeches from secession commissioners dispatched from several states to advocate for secession in other states. The arguments of these commissioners told a different story. These commissioners did not try to stir up Southern emotions by alluding to generic states' rights. They summoned every ounce of oratorical venom they could muster appealing to racial fears and bigotry. They passionately predicted that emancipation would result in race wars, collapse of Southern society, and rape of white women. Southern audiences enthusiastically accepted these ominous prophecies leading to secession.

Dew's epiphany resulted from quotes from secession commissioner's speeches and letters. These commissioners presented a consistent message, a sample of which follow.

Judge Harris to the joint session of the Georgia General Assembly:

> They have demanded, and now demand, equality between the white and negro races, under our Constitution; equality in representation, equality in the right of suffrage, equality in the honors and emoluments of office, equality in the social circle, equality in the rights of matrimony … freedom to the slave, but eternal degradation for you and for us. . . .

> Our fathers made this a government for the white man, rejecting the negro, as an ignorant, inferior, barbarian race, incapable of self-government, and not, therefore, entitled to be associated with the white man upon terms of civil, political, or social equality.

This new administration comes into power, under the solemn pledge to overturn and strike down this great feature of our Union, without which it would never have been formed, and to substitute in its stead their new theory of the universal equality of the black and white races.[11]

The triumph of this new theory of government destroys the property of the South, lays waste her fields, and inaugurates all the horrors of a San Domingo servile insurrection, consigning her citizens to assassinations and her wives and daughters to pollution and violation to gratify the lust of half-civilized Africans. . . . The slave-holder and non-slave-holder must ultimately share the same fate; all be degraded to a position of equality with free negroes, stand side by side with them at the polls, and fraternize in all the social relations of life, or else there will be an eternal war of races, desolating the land with blood, and utterly wasting all the resources of the country.[12]

Dew concluded, "slavery and race were absolutely critical elements" in the slavery debate prior to the Civil War.[13] In retrospect, the images used to stir Southern emotions appear irrational, but Southerners really feared these potential consequences. The war's conclusion did not alleviate these fears as proven by the reconstruction experience extending well into the twentieth century from lynching of blacks to segregation throughout the South.

Jefferson Davis

On January 21, 1861, Jefferson Davis gave his final speech before the Senate stating that Mississippi had seceded from the Union, and he would have to relinquish his seat.[14] Mississippi's rationale for secession was contained in one paragraph in that speech. It addressed use of the principles stated in Declaration of Independence in the slavery debate. The only right addressed was the right to own slaves.

It has been a conviction of pressing necessity, it has been a belief that we are to be deprived in the Union of the rights which our fathers bequeathed to us, which has brought Mississippi to her present decision. She has heard proclaimed the theory that all men are created free and equal, and this made the basis of an attack upon her social institutions; and the sacred Declaration of Independence has been invoked to maintain the position of the equality of the races. That Declaration of Independence is to be construed by the circumstances and purposes for which it was made. The communities were declaring their independence; the people of those communities were asserting that no man was born—to use the language of Mr. Jefferson—booted and spurred to ride over the rest of mankind; that men were created equal—meaning the men of the political community; that there was no divine right to rule; that no man inherited the right to govern; . . . but that all stations were equally within the grasp of each member of the body politic. These were the great principles they announced . . . . When our Constitution was formed, the same idea was rendered more palpable, for there we find provision made for that very class of persons as property; they were not put upon the footing of equality with white men—not even upon that of paupers and convicts; but, so far as representation was concerned, were discriminated against as a lower caste, only to be represented in the numerical proportion of three-fifths.

Since Davis is arguing the meaning and interpretation of the Declaration of Independence, it is prudent to recall exactly the words being debated. "We hold these truths to be self-evident, that all men are created equal, that they were endowed by their Creator with certain unalienable rights, that among these are life, liberty, and the pursuit of happiness." The fundamental principle of the Declaration is that God has granted mankind certain "unalienable rights." God is the only possible source for unalienable rights. All other rights can be abridged. Any discussion of this sentence must address this concept. Thomas Jefferson reiterated this concept in different words.

Can the liberties of a nation be thought secure when we have removed their only firm basis, a conviction in the minds of the people that these liberties are the gift of God? That they are not to be violated but by his wrath? Indeed, I tremble for my country when I reflect that God is just, that his justice cannot sleep forever. . . . The Almighty has no attribute which can take side with us in such a contest.[15]

Davis called the Declaration "sacred" to show his respect for the document. Yet, he chose to ignore its fundamental principle wishing to argue instead what the founding fathers had intended. Davis argued that the Declaration must "be construed by the circumstances and purposes for which it was made," and that the founders did not intend for slaves to participate in the right of liberty, something that was not universally true. Davis wished the Declaration said, "all men of the body politic are created equal." It did not. The argument of the Declaration would have been flawed with such wording. It would have argued that God had given only men of the "body politic" equal rights while denying those rights to others. The rights granted by God would depend on who was included in the "body politic" and could change over time. This concept of God is not supported by Scripture.

In his final speech, Davis makes no mention that the rights proclaimed in the Declaration come from God. If he had, he would have been forced to confess that only God could determine who enjoyed those rights. He ignored the rights named in the Declaration focusing instead on the Southern right to own slaves. Davis was arguing that God did not grant any unalienable rights to slaves without explaining how he reached that conclusion. His argument implied that there was a race of people born saddled and bridled ready to ride legitimately by the grace of God. Thomas Jefferson disagreed.

Davis argued that the Constitution condoned slavery. Abolitionists had recognized that also and rejected at least that portion of the Constitution. If the Declaration is correct in stating that the enumerated rights endowed by God are unalienable, then they cannot be abridged by any earthly document or authority including the Constitution. The Civil War can be viewed as a contest between the Declaration and Constitution. In the end, the Constitution had to be amended to agree with the Declaration.

Davis issued ten proclamations of humiliation, fasting, and prayer evincing belief in a God who intervened in the affairs of men. He ignored the possibility that God might intervene on behalf of slaves being denied rights he had granted. The Lost Cause myth overlooked that possibility also.

Confederates fancied themselves in a society which valued honor as depicted in Sir Walter Scott's romance novels. In *Ivanhoe*, Scott's most popular novel, heroic Ivanhoe, while in disguise, pledges to joist the evil knight, Sir Brian de Bois-Guilbert, on the field of honor. Everyone upon reading that pledge since the book's publication in 1819 has known that the joist would take place.[16] Sir Walter Scott would not, could not, write a book in which the protagonist makes a pledge only to hire lawyers to argue the meaning of words and query those present as to their understanding when its fulfillment becomes inconvenient. An honorable man makes a pledge to remove all doubt about the occurrence of the pledged event.

Whereas the Ivanhoe pledge was fictional, the Declaration pledge was real. Whereas the Ivanhoe pledge was oral, the Declaration pledge was written. Whereas the Ivanhoe pledge was spoken at a dinner, the Declaration pledge was addressed to "a candid world" and signed by representatives from each colony. Whereas the Ivanhoe pledge obligated two knights to joist, the Declaration pledge mandated the formation of a God-fearing government to protect God-endowed rights. Southerners were unanimous in their conviction that the Ivanhoe pledge could not be broken. They were just as unanimous in dismissing the Declaration pledge as inconsequential Jeffersonian hyperbole. It was altogether fitting and proper that a people who rejected the honor that comes from God to create their own honor standards should choose as their leader a person who revealed his profound ignorance of pledges.

If a man vow a vow unto the LORD, or swear an oath to bind his soul with a bond; he shall not break his word, he shall do according to all that proceedeth out of his mouth
(NUMBERS 30:2).

The Davis speech did not refer to the relative power of the state and federal government. Yankees never referenced the Declaration in a debate favoring a stronger federal government at the expense of state governments. The Davis speech was an obvious attempt to justify slavery while misrepresenting the clear meaning of the Declaration.

Confederate Constitution

The Confederate constitution copied the US Constitution with few modifications. Most of the modifications dealt with slavery or the right of secession. The Confederate Constitution, Article IV, Section 2:1,3 sought to avoid the issue raised by the Dred Scott case by ensuring that slaves could not claim any rights while traveling with their masters.[17] Article IV, Section 3:3 obviated the issue raised by the Republican platform by protecting slavery in any territories.[18]

Rewriting History

In a vain hope that historians would overlook inconsistencies, some Lost Cause advocates contradicted previous statements. On March 21, 1861, Alexander Stephens, Vice President of the Confederacy, said of the Confederate government that, "its foundations are laid, its cornerstone rests, upon the great truth that the negro is not equal to the white man; that slavery, subordination to the superior race, is his natural and moral condition." However, in his explanation of the war published in 1868 he said that the war "had its origin in opposing principles. ... It was a strife between the principles of Federation, on the one side, and Centralism, or Consolidation, on the other."[19]

Dew's research uncovered additional attempts to falsely justify Confederate objectives.

Passionate, unregenerate, unapologetic, unreconstructed—all these and more apply to Preston's remarks on this occasion. But so do words like 'conveniently forgetful,' 'strongly revisionist,' and ' purposely misleading.' Nowhere to be found are references to many of the arguments and descriptions he had used over and over again before the Virginia Convention in February 1861—things like 'the subject race…rising and murdering their masters' or 'the conflict between slavery and non-slavery is a conflict for life and death,' or his insistence that 'the South cannot exist without African slavery,' or his portrait of the 'fermenting millions' of the North as 'canting, fanatics, festering in the licentiousness of abolition and amalgamation.' All this was swept aside as Preston sought to paint the Civil War as a mighty struggle over differing concepts of constitutional liberty. Like Jefferson Davis and Alexander H. Stephens in their postwar writings, Preston was trying to reframe the causes of the conflict in terms that would be much more favorable to the South."[20]

To passionately advocate secession to preserve slavery before the war and argue that the war was fought over constitutional issues after the war is called lying.

Not every Southerner understood the necessity to rewrite history with Lost Cause assertions.

Captain Charles K. Maddox of the 7th Georgia was one of a handful of reunion speakers who linked secession with the preservation of slavery. In a 'widely praised' speech given in Decatur in 1890, Maddox declared that secession had not been 'a question of the union' but 'simply fought about niggers!' He reminded listeners that 'we fought for the supremacy of the white race in America; for civilization against abolition theories; the cause of truth against abolition prejudice; and the cause of common sense against the foulest errors that will ever astonish posterity.'[21]

Newspaper Accounts

Newspapers naturally joined in the secession debate. They also focused on the issue of slavery.

If in our present position of power and unitedness we have the raid of John Brown, and twenty towns burned down in Texas in one year by abolitionists [a widely circulated but false rumor], what will be the measures of insurrection and incendiarism which must follow our notorious and abject prostration to abolition rule in Washington . . .?[22]

Leonidas W. Spratt, editor of the *Charleston Mercury*, ridiculed the idea that secession was not over slavery in a letter addressed to the Honorable Mr. Perkins.[23] Spratt argued that slavery produced many profound, societal differences between North and South, which made conflict inevitable. The contentious debates and subsequent compromises leading up to secession concerned slavery, not states' rights. It never occurred to Spratt that subsistence farmers eking out the basic necessities could be persuaded to abandon families to fight for states' rights. Where were the passionate speeches and letters exhorting subsistence farmers to risk life, limb, and property to fight for states' rights? There were none. There is no record that people in the South were passionate about states' rights while those in the North were equally passionate about a strong central government.

Vocabulary

Using Chronicling America, I searched on the word "Republican" in South Carolina newspapers from 1861 through 1864. This database scanned in a number of papers and used optical character recognition to search on specific words. The software does not pick up every occurrence of a word. However, the search found 241 pages containing at least one occurrence of "Republican" or words beginning with this string such as "Republicans." Ninety-four times, the words were modified by the word "black." Twenty times the words were modified by another adjective, two of which were the word, "negro." There were no adjectives that related to Republicans wanting a stronger central government. South Carolina citizens could only conclude from this that the war was fought over slavery.

Republican Platform

The Republican platform of 1860 did not advocate federal superiority over state governments. In fact, the fourth article stated just the opposite.

> 4. That the maintenance inviolate of the rights of the states, and especially the right of each state to order and control its own domestic institutions according to its own judgment exclusively, is essential to that balance of powers on which the perfection and endurance of our political fabric depends; and we denounce the lawless invasion by armed force of the soil of any state or territory, no matter under what pretext, as among the gravest of crimes.[24]

Declarations of Secession

As the eleven seceding states voted on articles of secession, four of them issued declarations to express their grievances and justify their actions. South Carolina was the first state to secede. That state published a document titled "DECLARATION OF THE IMMEDIATE CAUSES WHICH INDUCE AND JUSTIFY THE SECESSION OF SOUTH CAROLINA FROM THE FEDERAL UNION." That document cited frequent violations of the Constitution as the underlying justification. The violation referenced was the failure of Northern states to capture and return escaped slaves.

We assert, that fourteen of the States have deliberately refused for years past to fulfil their constitutional obligations, and we refer to their own Statutes for the proof. The Constitution of the United States, in its 4th Article, provides as follows:

'No person held to service or labor in one State, under the laws thereof, escaping into another, shall, in consequence of any law or regulation therein, be discharged from such service or labor, but shall be delivered up, on claim of the party to whom such service or labor may be due.'

South Carolina continued by connecting their action to Lincoln's election.

A geographical line has been drawn across the Union, and all the States north of that line have united in the election of a man to the high office of President of the United States whose opinions and purposes are hostile to slavery.

South Carolina did not mention any other reason other than slavery for the decision to secede.

The opening sentences of Georgia's declaration relate to slavery.

The people of Georgia having dissolved their political connection with the Government of the United States of America, present to their confederates and the world the causes which have led to the separation. For the last ten years we have had numerous and serious causes of complaint against our non-slave-holding confederate States with reference to the subject of African slavery.

Mississippi's declaration consisted solely of a list of perceived abuses relating to slavery.

In the momentous step which our State has taken of dissolving its connection with the government of which we so long formed a part, it is but just that we should declare the prominent reasons which have induced our course.

Our position is thoroughly identified with the institution of slavery-- the greatest material interest of the world.

The Texas declaration clearly stated that the dominant factor in the secession decision was slavery.

In all the non-slave-holding States, in violation of that good faith and comity which should exist between entirely distinct nations, the people have formed themselves into a great sectional party, now strong enough in numbers to control the affairs of each of those States, based upon an unnatural feeling of hostility to these Southern States and their beneficent and patriarchal system of African slavery, proclaiming the debasing doctrine of equality of all men, irrespective of race or color—a doctrine at war with nature, in opposition to the experience of mankind, and in violation of the plainest revelations of Divine Law. . . .

In view of these and many other facts, it is meet that our own views should be distinctly proclaimed. . . .

That in this free government all white men are and of right ought to be entitled to equal civil and political rights; that the servitude of the African race, as existing in these States, is mutually beneficial to both bond and free, and is abundantly authorized and justified by the experience of mankind, and the revealed will of the Almighty Creator, as recognized by all Christian nations; while the destruction of the existing relations between the two races, as advocated by our sectional enemies, would bring inevitable calamities upon both and desolation upon the fifteen slave-holding states.

None of the documents provided an example of the Federal Government encroaching on states' rights. The Lost Cause myth never names the states' rights in dispute. However, there was a consensus that Northern states against their conscience should be compelled to comply with federal law. Conscience and the Declaration of

Independence convinced citizens of Northern states that the *Fugitive Slave Act* was immoral. Northerners who refused to participate in the sin of slavery by returning escaped slaves offended Confederate sensibilities. Each of the declarations names the reluctance of Free states to return escaped slaves as a major reason for secession.

Lost Cause advocates neither quote nor mention these documents because they do not support their myth. The truth about why the South fought the Civil War must be found in their statements made before and during the war, not afterwards. Those interested in knowing the truth need only examine the declarations of secession. No one is surprised by the absence of free states seceding to protect their states' rights because states' rights were not an issue. The declarations of secession are the most authoritative documents on the cause of the Civil War.

FAITHFUL SLAVES

Another argument used to deflect responsibility for the disastrous consequences of the Civil War was that African Americans were "faithful slaves," loyal to their masters and the Confederate cause and unprepared for the responsibilities of freedom. The implication was that blacks, unlike whites, did not valuing freedom. The burden to prove this contention lies with the South. If whites value freedom, why are blacks different? If blacks were contented, why did some run away from their family facing extreme punishment if apprehended? Why did the South insist on passage of the *Fugitive Slave Law* requiring Northerners to assist in slave apprehension? What caused the large assembly of blacks following Sherman's army? Why did so many slaves escape to the North as Northern armies drew near? How did the North recruit several black regiments to fight in the war? Why did the Southern commissioners argue that emancipation could lead to a race war?

Theodore Weld and the Grimke sisters wrote their book to confront this issue. No slave owners would have exchanged places with their slaves. We see no blacks currently seeking masters. Unless we hear from blacks that their ancestors were contented as slaves, we must add this assertion to the list of Confederate fabrications.

Obviously, not all slaves concurred with the Lost Cause description of their sentiments.

> It is a mistaken opinion that prevails in some quarters, that the slave does not understand the term—does not comprehend the idea of freedom. . . . They understand the privileges and exemptions that belong to it—that it would bestow upon them the fruits of their own labors, and that it would secure to them the enjoyment of domestic happiness. They do not fail to observe the difference between their own condition and the meanest white man's, and to realize the injustice of the laws which place it in his power not only to appropriate the profits of their industry, but to subject them to unmerited and unprovoked punishment, without remedy, or the right to resist, or to remonstrate.[25] I

came not to the conclusion, even once, that the southern slave, fed, clothed, whipped and protected by his master, is happier than the free colored citizen of the North.[26]

Slaves were divided into two basic classes: field slaves and house slaves. House slaves had more extensive contact with their masters which could result in a closer relationship. Mary Chesnut harangues on one of the results of this closer relationship in her diary.

God forgive us, but ours is a monstrous system, a wrong and an iniquity! Like the patriarchs of old, our men live all in one house with their wives and their concubines; and the mulattoes one sees in every family partly resemble the white children. Any lady is ready to tell you who is the father of all the mulatto children in everybody's household but her own. Those, she seems to think, drop from the clouds.[27]

House slaves led an easier life which was dependent on the continued favor of their owners. As such, masters knew their house slaves could be concealing their true sentiments to retain their favored positions. "It must be an awful bore to be deaf, dumb and blind, to go about with those sphinx-like faces. I often pity the awful self-control servants must practice."[28] "Not by one word or look do these slaves show that they know Sherman and freedom is at hand. They are more obedient and more considerate than ever, to me."[29]

Many slave owners wanted to believe their house slaves viewed them with affection. The reaction of Mary Chesnut and her friends when a slave murdered his owner revealed their ambivalence. In unguarded moments, slave owners revealed they did not believe this proposition any more than slaves believed it: "That night, Kate came into my room. She could not sleep. The thought of those black hands strangling and smothering Mrs. Witherspoon's grey head under the counterpane haunted her; we sat up and talked the long night through."[30] Forcing blacks to remain slaves against their will caused constant wariness among many slave owners. "Mrs. Chesnut, who is their good angel, is and has always been afraid of Negroes."[31] "He was in a state of abject fright because the Negroes show such exultation at the enemy's making good their entrance at Port Royal."[32]

SECESSION

The Lost Cause argument claims that secession was legal. Secession is not the same as revolution. Citizens always have the right to revolt as argued in the Declaration of Independence, "That whenever any form of government becomes destructive of these ends, it is the right of the people to alter or to abolish it." The colonies were in the act of revolting against England at the time the Declaration was drafted, and all who read it knew this was the intended meaning. When Confederates argued that they had the right to secede, they were claiming a legal right to leave the union peaceably without conflict.

Arguments about the legality of secession often referred to the Kentucky and Virginia Resolutions.[33] Both resolutions protested the *Alien and Sedition Acts*. Thomas Jefferson authored the Kentucky Resolution while James Madison wrote the Virginia Resolution.

Secessionists usually focus on Jefferson's statements which endorse the concept of nullification, "whensoever the general government assumes undelegated powers, its acts are unauthoritative, void, and of no force." Jefferson continued by arguing that states had the legal right to determine which federal laws were illegal and what actions should be taken to cure the violation. For Confederates, this would include secession.

However, Madison and Jefferson did not speak with equal authority on the Constitution. Madison is considered the father of the Constitution. Jefferson was ambassador to France during the Constitutional Convention and was in France during much of the time when the Articles of Confederation were in force. As such, he did not experience firsthand the weakness of a Confederation of states and participated in none of the debates or discussions.

Those arguing for secession implied that both resolutions agreed on this principle. This was false. The Virginia Resolution merely called for support from other states to oppose the *Alien and Sedition Acts*, making no mention of nullification. Madison addressed the question of nullification in a letter to Edward Everett in August of 1830.[34] He pointed out that the people of the individual states ratified the federal Constitution just as they ratified the state constitutions. As such, state and federal constitutions obtained their authority from the same source and, thus, were equal in authority in their respective spheres. The Constitution provided remedies when disputes arose over authority. Citizens could elect new representatives in the House and Senate. States could appeal to the Supreme Court. As a final resort, the Constitution could be amended. In ratifying the Constitution, citizens agreed to accept only the means for settling disputes contained in that document.

For those areas where authority was granted to the Federal Government, the Constitution declares that the Federal Government is supreme. Article VI, of the Constitution says: "This Constitution, and the Laws of the United States which shall be made in Pursuance thereof; and all Treaties made, or which shall be made, under the Authority of the United States, shall be the supreme Law of the Land." Obviously, federal law could not be the supreme law of the land if states had the authority to nullify it. Knowing that disputes would arise over jurisdiction, the Constitution also identified the institution intended to settle disputes. Speaking about the Supreme Court, Article III, section 2 of the Constitution says: "The judicial Power shall extend to all Cases, in Law and Equity, arising under this Constitution, the Laws of the United States . . ." Having identified the Supreme Court as the institution with authority to settle disputes involving jurisdiction, the citizens excluded all other institutions including the states.

Madison rejected the concept of nullification arguing that "a uniform authority of the laws, is in itself a vital principle." If individual states could decide on the legality of laws, these laws would be enforced unequally. Madison assured Everett that drafters of the Constitution did not intend such a purpose and never endorsed the concept of nullification.

The concept of nullification was tested in the 1830s when South Carolina attempted to nullify tariffs. President Andrew Jackson threatened to use military force to enforce federal law. South Carolina backed down as tariff rates were reduced in a compromise.

Those opposed to nullification and secession, argued that both policies would result in the eventual destruction of the government.

> Unquestionably the States have the powers and rights reserved to them in and by the National Constitution; but among these surely are not included all conceivable powers, however mischievous or destructive, but, at most, such only as were known in the world at the time as governmental powers; and certainly a power to destroy the government itself had never been known as a governmental, as a merely administrative power.[35]

The framers of the Constitution, knowing the consequences of these policies, would never have authorized them.

The Northern position was that secession was illegal. This position was enforced in the conditions of surrender by forbidding the South to pay off

Confederate debts. Contracts entered into for illegal purposes are unenforceable. By requiring the South to default on war debts, the North was requiring the South to admit that secession was illegal.

Southern apologists argue the South was justified in seceding because the North had not complied with the Fugitive Slave Act. However, there is never any excuse for not complying with a covenant with God because God always fulfills his part of the covenant perfectly. In the case of the Declaration of Independence, God completed his part of the covenant by ensuring that the United States obtained independence from Great Britain. Any state joining the United States assumed the obligation of conforming to the Declaration covenant. No act of men or nations could annul that covenant or avoid consequences for failing to comply.

SOUTHERN SAINTS

Another component of the Lost Cause myth was bestowing sainthood on Confederate soldiers, women, and, especially, Robert E. Lee. During the last week of May 1890, Confederate zealots met to commemorate a statue of Robert E. Lee. Archer Anderson delivered a keynote address on the 29th, saying he

> saw in the commanding general the rare combination of Christian virtues and heroic nature of Lee and the Confederacy. Like many spokesmen for the Lost Cause, Anderson moved beyond a narrow justification of the South's actions during the war. He portrayed Lee as a

man of action, intelligence, and vigor who offered a model of behavior for Southerners trying to adapt to the realities of the New South.[36]

Randolph H. McKim, an officer on Brig. Gen. George H. Stuart's staff and later a leading Episcopal priest, wrote of Lee. 'from the day when he publicly gave himself to the service of God in old Christ Church, Alexandria, he lived not to himself but to God and his fellow men.' Lee was, McKim continued, infused 'by the Christ-like spirit of self-sacrifice,' and 'the sign of the Cross was upon his life.'

Since the Son of Man stood upon the Mount and saw all the kingdoms of the earth and the glory thereof stretched before him, and turned away from them to the agony and bloody sweat of Gethsemane, and to the Cross of Calvary beyond, no follower of the meek and lowly Saviour can have undergone more trying ordeal, or met it with higher spirit of heroic sacrifice.'[37]

Lee may very well have been a man of action, but logic demands we connect the unrighteous cause of the war with those who fought it. Mr. McKim failed to mention one significant difference between Jesus and Robert E. Lee. Jesus was doing the will of the Father; Lee was fighting against God's will.

Confederate insistence on Lee's sainthood was not based on Lee's generalship. In their hearts, Confederates believed that they could only qualify for sainthood if they were fighting for a righteous cause. The effort by Confederate apologists to convince posterity of Confederate Christian virtue was another effort to argue that Confederates fought for such a cause.

Some former slaves expressed skepticism concerning the bona fides of "Marse Robert" for canonization:

Former slave and abolitionist Frederick Douglass complained bitterly that he could scarcely find a northern newspaper "that is not filled with nauseating flatteries of the late Robert E. Lee," whose military accomplishments in the name of a "bad cause" seemed somehow to entitle him "to the highest place in heaven."[38]

Douglass labored under the biblical perception that God bestowed sainthood upon those who adhered to moral principles.

Similar accolades were spoken over Confederate soldiers.

Since he bore those marks, the martyred Sam Davis—the South's Nathan Hale—served as the ultimate model of the common soldier. In the young Tennessean, hanged by Union soldiers as a spy in 1864, postwar Confederates found an emblem of valor, honor, and sacrifice which contained all their images of the Confederate fighting man. His last words, vowing his loyalty to his comrades and his refusal to inform on them, were compared to those of Jesus: 'Greater love hath no man than this, that he lay down his life for his friends.' Described as one of God's 'own instruments' who, 'touched by the hand divine . . .rose from the gallows to the crown,' Sam Davis became another Confederate Christ:

On Calvary the Son of God died with cruel nails driven through his quivering flesh, the crown of thorns pressing down on his agonized brow, and since then the cross has been the Christian's sign in every land; and which of us has the right to say that He who created the earth and the sky and every living thing on sea and land, whose mysteries baffle, but whose providence is over all, could give the Son of Mary to teach men how to live could not also give this son of Tennessee to teach men how to die?[39]

Somehow, the blood of slaves drawn by the lash failed to baptize and sanctify Dixie's soil in any way.

Lost Cause apologists tell us what great Christians Robert E. Lee, Confederate soldiers, and Southern women were. This position poses a dilemma. We know God is not schizophrenic. He is not confused about the institution of slavery as it was practiced in the South, and its relation to the Declaration of Independence. If the Declaration of Independence was indeed a covenant with God and the Civil War a judgment in response, then the war was caused directly by God. No human wisdom could have averted that judgment. The Christianity of those who opposed God was vain and anyone fighting to preserve slavery was fighting against the will of God and was a deluded Christian at best, not a saint.

HERE'S THE DEAL

Refusing to Hear

Civil War studies should begin by questioning the morality of slavery. Was the Declaration of Independence a covenant with God? The answer to these questions affects the interpretation of events. The Lost Cause myth was developed to avoid answering these questions. As long as slavery remained legal, the Declaration was not an enlightened statement of moral principles but a declaration of national hypocrisy.

Southern apologists denied that slavery had any moral implications both before[40] and after the war.[41] In the early 1840s, House of Representatives rules went so far as to prohibit all discussion of slavery.

> 21. No petition, memorial, resolution, or other paper praying the abolition of slavery in the District of Columbia, or any State or Territory, or the slave trade between the States or Territories of the United States, in which it now exists, shall be received by this House, or entertained in any way whatever.[42]

Apparently, Southerners hoped the subject could be avoided and slavery continued indefinitely. However, slavery was a moral issue for abolitionists. They felt they were doing God's will and could not quit. By disregarding moral arguments before the war, slavery advocates postponed the issue until it exploded in armed conflict.

By the time the Civil War began, most Southerners had successfully deluded themselves into believing a benevolent God created blacks to be slaves to serve them. They believed God was obligated to answer their prayers to assist them in killing Yankees. Following their defeat that, "ravaged their military-age male population, vastly altered their physical landscape and economic infrastructure, and destroyed their slave-based social system,"[43] they continued to believe in their righteousness. They felt God had misled and abandoned them by failing to grant their petitions. They continued to ignore moral implications of defeat.

The South's ultimate defeat left Confederates confused and bewildered. As they ignored the Declaration of Independence earlier, they now ignored the implications of the war's outcome. However, they knew others would attribute their defeat to God's judgment. They immediately began developing a narrative to refute that conclusion. After the war, they extended their resume of character flaws to include brazen liars by proclaiming the myth of the Lost Cause in a futile attempt to rewrite history.

Why Should We Care
With such obvious discrepancies in Lost Cause premises, why did Confederates promote them so passionately?

What has prevented the truth from reaching 62 percent of the population? The Civil War exacted a staggering toll on a personal level. Children lost fathers they had been taught to admire and imitate. Wives lost beloved husbands and found themselves responsible for providing for themselves and families. Parents proudly watched sons enlist to defend a cause they endorsed. Many soldiers who survived battles and field hospitals returned to civilian life to earn a living with only one arm or leg. Confederates faced a dilemma. They desperately needed to believe that their cause was worth the sacrifice at a time when most of the world viewed slavery as immoral.

Obituaries provide a candid, edifying view into Confederate souls. All obituaries sought comfort while mourning the loss of loved ones. They referred to the hope of a happier life in heaven. The word *martyr* was occasionally used: "Thus has passed away, in the 27th year of his age, one of the noble army of our Christian patriots, who are fighting the battles of our freedom, and enrolling their names among its blessed martyrs."[44] "chivalry will write thy name a hero, virtue claim thee as a devotee, and thy country mourn thee as a martyr."[45] "It may with propriety, be said of this youthful martyr, he fell a gallant soldier of his country and rose a triumphant soldier of the Cross; he fell in the sacred cause of freedom. . . ."[46] Martyrdom claims encountered the same problem as Lee's hagiography. Use of the word, *martyr* implied that the sacrifice of loved ones was worthwhile because they died for a noble cause. To label slain loved ones *martyrs* was equivalent to proclaiming the righteousness of the Confederate cause without fear of contradiction. No one was going to argue with survivors about the qualifications of Southern casualties for martyrdom.

The absence of articles eulogizing the deceased for defending slavery reveals that despite passionate and heated arguments defending their institution, despite paid clerics providing theological justification, Confederates remained ambivalent. Confederates must have been troubled somewhere deep in their psyche, by the inconsistencies of their theology. Obituaries confirm that Harriet Beecher Stowe was correct when she had her character, St. Clare, say after all the Southern arguments, "neither they nor the world believe in it one particle the more." Confederate senators and congressmen may have threatened secession over slavery and eventually seceded over that issue while beating their fellow Congressmen for debating it, but family and friends could not bring themselves to admit that loved ones had died defending it. Southern churches following the Lost Cause example of self-justification refused to admit they split from Northern counterparts over slavery. They attributed church splits to issues involving "church governance and the proper purview of ecclesiastical bodies."[47]

Confederate clergy assertions of righteousness said something profoundly significant about their concept of God. They believed God approved slavery, that he created the black race for perpetual servitude. Their concept proclaimed that God created a black race that was not fully human and had not endowed them with the same inalienable rights that he had given the white race. Admitting this view was incorrect would mean departed loved ones encountered a God they had slandered.

Northerners were aware of the moral dilemma facing Southern society. Some Northern clergy believed their Southern counterparts were the most vocal secessionists and dogmatic apologists for slavery in the Confederacy. These clerical heretics had misrepresented God leading Southern society into a disastrous war.[48] Their opinion of Southern laity was more sympathetic, viewing them as poorly educated and deceived. This conviction motivated Northerners to plan missionary outreaches to rescue deluded Southern citizenry from moral decay by preaching on the humanity of blacks and their rights to liberty. This attempted moral reconstruction failed. White culture was not ready to admit to being duped. Their clerics had spoken as demanded. Admitting they were snookered carried with it the unacceptable implication that loved ones had died for an ignoble cause. Finding the proffered dose of reality bitter, they found the tenets of the Lost Cause more to their taste.[49] People who believed slavery was the will of God could believe anything.

A judgment of the morality of slavery is required to accurately understand the motivation and development of the Lost Cause. Even though some refused to admit it, Confederates lost the worldwide debate over the morality of slavery before the Civil War began. The emancipation of the slaves after the war made the theological justification of slavery indefensible.

Furthermore, the existence of the Lost Cause narrative is implicit admission that slavery is immoral. If the morality of slavery were not settled theology, Southerners could admit they fought to preserve it and continue their arguments defending it.

The United States is caught in a dilemma. The logical consequences of a moral decision are grave indeed. Americans, and particularly Southerners, want to honor Confederate soldiers. However, the immorality of slavery requires us to put an asterisk after the names of Confederate soldiers acknowledging that they fought for an immoral cause. Ultimately, the Lost Cause myth developed for the same reason all myths develop—to avoid the ugly truth. Southern honor could not brook such harsh and blatant honesty. Confederates preferred to believe their cause was righteous. This belief led inevitably to the conclusion that God abandoned noble worthies defending their righteous cause.

Southern clergy defended slavery against abolitionist charges. They forced denominations to split over this issue initiating the sectional schism. The moral judgment of slavery implies these clergy mislead Southern society facilitating the most destructive war in the nation's history. They misrepresented God to both the free and enslaved. Southern clergy's passionate defense of an immoral institution for decades revealed that they were more interested in retaining their position and the praise of men than the truth. Of course, not all clergy compromised. Some moved North because they felt slavery was immoral. However, most stayed and, rather than face obvious implications of defeat, developed and supported fictitious propositions to avoid responsibility. Southern clergy chose to defend their righteousness implicitly censuring God for abandoning them. The war's outcome coupled with Confederate belief in their righteousness caused many to question their faith. South Carolina clergyman, John L. Girardear, blamed Satan for his congregation's distrust in prayer.[50] This raises the fundamental epistemological question troubling mankind ever since the Garden, "How do we know truth?" While a universally accessible source of truth remains unidentified, we can eliminate clergy as a reliable option.

Today's Lost Cause apologists demonstrate the same tenacity in defending the indefensible, Confederate righteousness, as the Southern clergy did during the war. What harm does it do if 62 percent of the citizens of this country are confused about the Confederate motivation to secede? Why do we study history at all if it is merely a smorgasbord of fantasies from which everyone is free to choose the least offensive? We study history so we will not repeat the mistakes of the past. If the study of history is to achieve this objective, we must acknowledge truth, even if it offends Southern sensibilities.

In addition to accurate facts, to be beneficial history requires accurate interpretation as well. "The historian does not merely tell a story—what has happened—he interprets the story also by attempting to explain why it happened."[51] Different historians can derive different stories from the same data. The reader is then required to determine which story best explains all relevant facts. Some authors writing about the Lost Cause while allowing that some tenets are false have maintained that some were at least partially true.[52] However, if the Declaration of Independence is a covenant with God, all the tenets are obviously false because the motive behind this narrative is to eliminate any record of divine influence.

The proposition that the Declaration of Independence is a covenant with God is one explanation of events. The Lost Cause is another. Both explanations cannot be true. Whatever narrative one chooses to explain events leading up to and through the Civil War will dictate the lessons learned.

It is the nature of mankind to delay decisions perceived to cause discomfort or danger. Antebellum Southerners found abolitionists' arguments from the Declaration inconvenient. The vast majority thought they could ignore those arguments without repercussions. This sequence of events began by Confederate rationalization of slavery, ignoring the obvious moral implications. There are grave consequences for ignoring moral issues. They cannot be successfully ignored forever.

Perhaps Confederates felt the founding fathers made a bad bargain. Perhaps they figured the colonies could have won independence without divine favor. That was 80 some years ago. Surely, God would not hold them to a pledge made by men who had all died long ago. However, God had given an unmistakable warning that he considered the Declaration a covenant with the simultaneous deaths of Adams and Jefferson. Confederates ignored the covenant made by the founding fathers and could not understand why God ignored their fasting and prayers. Many still choose to passionately defend the righteousness of Robert E. Lee oblivious to the fact that they are simultaneously declaring their God to be either indifferent or impotent.

Everyone should be extremely careful about making vows to God, but surely the founding fathers were safe in making this vow. This was not some onerous requirement leading the fledgling nation toward bankruptcy. Surely, all reasonable citizens would agree that these very basic rights required governmental protection. Even if slavery were a moral institution for the rest of the world, it could never be one for the United States. The nation's founding document pledged our lives, fortunes, and sacred honor to create a government guaranteeing the God-granted inalienable rights of everyone. The United States is obligated to honor that pledge.

When thou shalt vow a vow unto the LORD thy God, thou shalt not slack to pay it: for the LORD thy God will surely require it of thee; and it would be sin in thee
(DEUTERONOMY 23:21).

CHAPTER TEN

CONFIRMATION

That this is a rebellious people, lying children, children that will not hear the law of the LORD:

Which say to the seers, See not; and to the prophets, Prophesy not unto us right things, speak unto us smooth things, prophesy deceits:

Get you out of the way, turn aside out of the path, cause the Holy One of Israel to cease from before us

(ISAIAH 30:9–11),

THE INADVERTENT, UNACKNOWLEDGED COVENANT

The Declaration of Independence is the founding document for the United States. Its drafting and ratification not only birthed a new nation; it also codified new principles for founding a nation based on freedom and equality. Despite the gravity of these contributions, the true importance of the document has yet to be fully understood and appreciated.

The final paragraph contains important information which must be comprehended to appreciate the significance of the Declaration.

> We, therefore, the Representatives of the United States of America, in general Congress assembled, appealing to the Supreme Judge of the world for the rectitude of our intentions, do, in the name and by the authority of the good people of these Colonies, solemnly publish and declare that ... they have full power to ... contract alliance. . . . And for the Support of this Declaration, with a firm reliance on the protection of Divine Providence, we mutually pledge to each other our lives, our fortunes, and our sacred honor.

Colonies voted on ratification, not delegates. The signers did not decide for themselves to attend the Continental Congress. They were selected by colonies. The 56 signers did not enter into a compact to win independence. Colonies entered into such an agreement. Citizens universally perceived themselves as participants in this covenant to fight for independence.

An understanding of these points is vital to a proper understanding of the concluding pledge. Beyond all dispute, the pronoun, "we," in the Declaration refers to colonies, not signers. The entire document must be read with this understanding. If the pledge had been between the signers, it would not have obligated colonies. However, as a compact between colonies, it obligated all citizens and remains in effect as long as the country exists.

The pledge addressed the ongoing conflict with Great Britain. It demonstrated unity and resolve. It assured individual colonies that their fellow colonies would expend the effort necessary to gain independence. If each colony met its obligations, no colony would be forced to bear a disproportionate share of the military and financial burden.

To comply with the Declaration, political leaders of each colony would have to make the decisions, provide the leadership, and commit the resources of their respective colonies to support the revolution. If leaders failed, the electorate was responsible for replacing them. The Declaration was published "in the name and by the authority of the good people of these Colonies." Since the citizens held final authority, they were ultimately accountable for ensuring their colonies fulfilled their responsibilities.

Although the ongoing conflict was foremost in everyone's minds, the stated objective of the Declaration was not merely independence from Great Britain. When colonies appealed to God "for the rectitude" of their intentions, the end result anticipated the creation of a government based upon the principle that God has endowed everyone with equal rights. Thus, citizen's responsibilities did not terminate with the war's end. Constant vigilance was required to ensure continued compliance.

In appealing to God to judge the rectitude of their intentions and asserting a firm reliance on the protection of Divine Providence, the Declaration expressed an expectation and anticipation that God would intervene to implement and enforce the covenant, including judgment of those who failed to comply. The rectitude of their stated intentions was honorable. Implementation was judged faulty.

Although colonies were the parties to the compact, they could not forfeit lives, et cetera. The Declaration, in effect, obligated citizens to ensure that each colony complied with stated conditions, committing them to forfeit their lives, fortunes, and honor if the colony failed. Signers of the Declaration were parties to the covenant as citizens of their respective colonies. They had additional responsibility since they debated and voted on the Declaration. Adams and Jefferson bore the greatest responsibility as the primary contributors to the document.

The covenant did not expire upon the signers' deaths. It continues with the states and extends to all states and, by implication, all citizens of states joining the union. The terms of this covenant continue in existence today. Covenants in the Bible extend for many generations. When Moses brought the Ten Commandments down from Mount Sinai, he and the Israelites of that time instituted a covenant still affecting those who seek to live by those commandments.

Historians have debated the relative importance of events occurring around July 4, 1776. While pointing out that the Declaration was not signed on the fourth, they remain oblivious to the true significance of the document.[1] Whereas there were many events involved in the birth of the nation, the ratification of the Declaration formed a covenant with God.

Slavery advocates and abolitionists were equally ignorant of their covenant obligations. However, ignorance did not guarantee noncompliance. Moral conduct would have resulted in obedience. Abolitionists opposed slavery on moral grounds and could not understand how those who considered themselves Christians could defend or ignore slavery's brutality.

SINS OF COMMISSION VERSES OMISSION

Therefore to him that knoweth to do good, and doeth it not, to him it is sin
(JAMES 4:17).

The Declaration does not merely promise that the government would not usurp rights. It pledged a government to secure or protect God-endowed rights. When the government failed to secure the God-endowed right of liberty for slaves, it failed in its responsibility and was guilty of a sin of omission. The nation blatantly manifested its moral oversight while celebrating its Jubilee. The *New York Post* did not mention any opposition towards slavery at a time when biblically literate citizens would naturally remember and consider its offensiveness. Since the brutality of slavery raised moral issues, one would expect the church to lead the opposition to this practice. Unfortunately, the church was compromised.

Southern clergy had compromised on the slavery issue to obtain access to Southerners and their slaves. Denominational ties made Northern clergy complicit in this compromise. As a part of their compromise, Southern clergy vehemently defended slavery in denominational gatherings, strongly resenting defamatory statements against that institution by Northern counterparts. As a result, most opposition to slavery had evaporated in the major denominations as the nation's Jubilee approached. Quakers were a rare exception.

The author of the Declaration of Independence, Thomas Jefferson, in his departing speech to the nation read on the day of his death alluded to the lack of moral leadership by the church, "the mass of mankind has not been born with saddles on their backs, nor a favored few, booted and spurred ready to ride them legitimately, by the grace of God." The last phrase, "legitimately, by the grace of God," mocked what Jefferson saw as the prevailing national sentiment.

The Bible mandated that slaves must be freed every fifty years. The simultaneous deaths of Adams and Jefferson on the nation's Jubilee implied that God had given the United States fifty years to free the slaves. As the grace period for resolving the slavery issue expired, God raised up a small cadre of abolitionists. These people had the rare combination of DNA and life-molding experiences to qualify them to be social activists. Those society traditionally label leaders longingly aspire to speak to large audiences convincing them to pursue comfort and affluence. By contrast, social activists typically labored in obscurity. Rather than basking in public approval, they sought conflict. They sought issues where they could use moral authority to oppose majority views.

One of the primary influences in Garrison's development was Quaker Benjamin Lundy who continued his opposition to slavery throughout this period. He operated a one-man newspaper, the *Genius of Universal Emancipation*, where William Lloyd Garrison worked for a time. Garrison judged Lundy's paper a "little dingy sheet" overflowing with "earnestness and zeal."[2] On March 17, 1826, William Lloyd Garrison purchased his own newspaper, the *Essex Courant*. As the fiftieth anniversary of the Declaration of Independence approached, God was preparing him for the battle to come.[3] Garrison would become a leader in the abolitionist movement as editor of *The Liberator*.

A number of social issues competed for the attention of social activists as Garrison began his newspaper career including slavery, temperance, gambling, dueling, and the vote for women. With no concept of the Declaration pledge and God's subsequent warning, Garrison somehow identified slavery as the dominant problem.

> Between 1826 and 1829, Boston framed the path that led him [Garrison] from a benign interest in human betterment to a burning concentration on racial injustice, from a diffuse ideology of benevolent uplift to the pointed one of immediate abolition of slavery, and from the limited horizons of a small-town printer to the ambitious universe of a crusading national editor.[4]

As Garrison began to denounce slavery, he quickly realized that politicians would not assist in mobilizing public opinion. They never lead on issues with minimal public support. Politicians could never get elected by taking such positions, and they always focus on getting elected.[5]

Abolitionists found that most clergy were disinclined to preach against slavery also. Everyone who sought public fame and approval suffered from the same weakness. Clergy savored congregants' approval and, therefore, opposed any issue that would disturb their peace.[6] When Garrison planned an abolition speech in 1830, all the Boston churches refused his request for a venue.[7] The search for a location in 1837 met with the same result. "Every church in Boston closed its doors against the MAS [Massachusetts Anti-Slavery Society]..."[8] "When Garrison began his attacks on slavery, and incidentally on the churches, all the power of Methodism was mustered in opposition."[9]

This revelation frustrated abolitionists. "The abolition of slavery had to be a moral endeavor before it could be a political one."[10] Frederick Douglass expressed displeasure with the established church while addressing the significance of the Fourth of July to slaves. "From what quarter, ... has proceeded a fire so deadly upon our ranks, during the last two years, as from the Northern pulpit? . . . the anti-slavery movement in this country will cease to be an anti-church movement, when the church of this country shall assume a favorable, instead of a hostile position towards that movement."[11] Unfortunately, those who claimed to be moral leaders refused to lead on this issue and, in fact, openly opposed abolition as long as it remained unpopular. Although many abolitionists came out of the Second Great Awakening and based their activism on religious principles, cleric's opposition to abolition caused many to distrust the established church.

Politicians and clergy loved to be addressed by titles denoting honor and authority. The perceived opinion of peers had threatened these titles and neutered those holding them.[12] The small band of abolitionists had no titles. Society bestowed upon them no honor. They were free to express moral convictions.[13]

> **For the eyes of the LORD run to and fro throughout the whole earth, to shew himself strong in the behalf of them whose heart is perfect toward him**
> (2 CHRONICLES 16:9A).

When the war began, abolitionists recognized the possibility of Divine judgment. Garrison observed that the nation's indifference to the slave's condition resembled that of Israel in Jeremiah.

> **Therefore thus saith the LORD; Ye have not hearkened unto me, in proclaiming liberty, every one to his brother, and every man to his neighbour: behold, I proclaim a liberty for you, saith the LORD, to the sword, to the pestilence, and to the famine; and I will make you to be removed into all the kingdoms of the earth**
> (JEREMIAH 34:17).

This text was used to preach scores of abolitionist messages in the early months of the war.[14] While Southerners broke the Declaration pledge by actively defending and promoting slavery, Northerners broke it by ignoring slavery. Both merited judgment.

DUELING VIRTUES

The slavery debate revolved around fundamental religious issues. In his second inaugural address, Abraham Lincoln noted that citizens of both the North and South were praying that God would favor their cause.

> Both read the same Bible and pray to the same God, and each invokes His aid against the other. It may seem strange that any men should dare to ask a just God's assistance in wringing their bread from the sweat of other men's faces, but let us judge not, that we be not judged. The prayers of both could not be answered. That of neither has been answered fully.

Both believed their cause was righteous. Both sides could not be right.

In referring to those who were praying, Lincoln left out the slaves. It could be argued that the prayers of slaves were answered fully. The North's objective at the beginning of the war was reunification of the nation. If the North had achieved early battlefield successes leading to rapid reunification, slaves would have remained in bondage. The Emancipation Proclamation changed the character of the war. After January 1, 1863 freedom for slaves became an additional outcome of Northern victory.[15]

EMANCIPATION

When Civil War broke out, many abolitionists withheld their support because the North lacked an antislavery objective. Naturally, they fought to make abolition a goal. During this time, Lincoln's administration and a substantial portion of the Republican Party denied that the North fought to abolish slavery. In his July 1861 address to Congress, Lincoln justified the war as "military suppression of rebellion." He argued that elections in a democracy should not be overruled by armed rebellion. *The Methodist* argued correctly that "The president, his counsellors, and Congress have each and all steadily resisted the clamors of the zealots who have urged that emancipation be made the direct object of the war."[16] Jacob Ritner understood that he was fighting to preserve the union when he enlisted for 100 days. "But, if I can be of any use in sustaining our country and our flag, I shall consider myself well paid. My only regret is that a set of scoundrels and thieves has made it necessary to resort to such means to preserve our glorious institutions."[17]

Abolitionists realized that the Northern defeat at Bull Run in July 1861 in a twisted way enhanced the antislavery cause. In light of Lincoln's expressed position and Northern sentiment, a rapid Northern victory would have left slavery intact. As the war progressed, this attitude began to shift. In August, Congress passed a *Confiscation Act*, permitting the seizure of Confederate property including slaves used to aid the rebellion. By the end of the month, General Fremont issued an order emancipating all slaves in Missouri. Lincoln quickly repealed this order demonstrating clearly that emancipation was not yet a Northern objective. Abolitionists were furious. Not only did it continue Northern recognition of slavery, but they felt it would prolong the war.

Abolitionists continued their work of enlightening public opinion through speeches, pamphlets, newspapers, and petition drives. Without Southern representation, Congress passed several antislavery bills including the prohibition of slavery in the territories and Washington DC, more effective suppression of the slave trade, and recognition of Haiti and Liberia. However, Lincoln once again reinforced the North's single objective by repealing another emancipation order issued by General Hunter. In August 1862, Lincoln told newspaper editor, Horace Greeley, "if he could save the Union without freeing a single slave, he would do it."[18] The *Chicago Times* described a committee of Christian men who met with the President as "The religious community of Chicago" who "believe that the country is now suffering under Divine judgments for the sin of oppression, and who favor the adoption of a memorial to the President of the United States, urging him to issue a decree of emancipation, as a sign of national repentance as well as a military necessity."[19]

Lincoln initially proposed an emancipation proclamation to his cabinet who advised him to wait for a Northern victory. As the Battle of Antietam Creek approached, Lincoln sought divine confirmation regarding emancipation which he later revealed to his cabinet as recorded by Secretary of the Navy Gideon Welles.

> He had made a vow, a covenant, that if God gave us the victory in the approaching battle, he would consider it an indication of divine will and that it was his duty to move forward in the cause of emancipation. It might be thought strange that he had in this way submitted the disposal of matters when the way was not clear to his mind what he should do. God had decided this question in favor of the slaves. He was satisfied that it was right, was confirmed and strengthened in this action by the vow and the results.[20]

When Union forces under McClellan successfully halted Lee's Northern advance, Lincoln announced he would emancipate all slaves in states remaining in rebellion on January 1, 1863. When the Emancipation Proclamation was released on that date, abolitionists rejoiced that the North had added the objective of eliminating slavery. As the proclamation concluded, Lincoln invoked "the gracious favor of Almighty God." Lincoln was unaware that with this proclamation the North was once again in compliance with the covenant formed by the colonies in the Declaration. The favor of Almighty God could once again grace their endeavors.

As Northerners began to fight for slave freedom, they were fighting in support of the principles of the Declaration while Southerners fought against them. Divine approval upon the North began to manifest from this point forward. In his book, *The Cause Lost, Myths and Realities of the Confederacy*, William Davis notes the change in fortunes for both North and South between 1862 and 1863. Confederate enlistments in 1862 were more successful than Northern recruitment. The trend reversed in 1863. "It seems evident that something was at work in 1863 that was not there in 1862, and that something was staying the natural fall-off of enlistments in the North while failing to stop it in the South."[21] Desertions for the Army of the Potomac were 100,000 for 1862 and fell to 56,000 in 1863. Confederate desertion rate rose 18 per cent from 1862 to 1863. Southern men began enlisting in the Union army. "Thus, by every measurable indicator available, the sentiment of the people at home and of the men in the field shows the dramatic shift from a depressed and faltering North against an invigorated and confident South at the end of 1862 to a near-exact reversal a year later."[22] These notable reversals occurred despite Southern dominance on the battlefield to that point. On the evening of May 2, 1863, Stonewall Jackson was shot by his own men. He died May 10th.

Confederates responded to abolitionists' attacks from the Declaration of Independence referring to the citizens' right to reject governments. In this case,

Confederates rejected government which threatened to comply with its pledged obligation to protect God-endowed rights. This attitude was reflected in an opinion published in *The Daily Dispatch*, Richmond, Virginia, in the July 4 issue.

> The Declaration of Independence, fringed and gilt with certain transcendentalisms, imbibed from the French philosophy of the day, with which Mr. Jefferson and his contemporaries had become somewhat inoculated, set forth the popular rights for which we are this day battling. The main principles it asserted the Yankees never could approve. It is that Governments "derive their just powers from the consent of the governed."

> The Yankees think they have a right to govern the Southern people against their consent. They have desecrated both the day and the principles which it commemorates, and the very best way in which we can celebrate it is by whipping them. A good victory over them would be the best tribute we could offer in the memory of the signers of the Declaration. Let us pray for one.[23]

The day this philosophy was printed, Confederates surrendered Vicksburg giving the North control of the Mississippi, and Lee began his retreat from Gettysburg. It was the turning point in the war. Reverend Elliott expressed his perception of Confederate morale after these defeats: "What is it then, which spread over the Confederate States, so suddenly without any adequate reason, such a robe of darkness?"[24]

The outcome of the battle of Gettysburg appeared in doubt to those who fought it. Both the Northern and Southern commanders felt that Confederates would win the battle if they could control Little Roundtop. The Northern commander, Joshua Lawrence Chamberlain, was ordered to defend it at all costs. After five Confederate assaults, Chamberlain's regiment was out of ammunition. They could not withstand another assault. They could not retreat. Chamberlain ordered his men to fix bayonets and charge, routing Southern troops.

Just as God announced to the nation that it was not complying with its covenant with the simultaneous deaths of Adams and Jefferson on July 4, 1826, God announced that the Union was once again in compliance with the simultaneous defeats of the Confederates at Gettysburg and Vicksburg on July 4, 1863, the Fourth of July following the Emancipation Proclamation. It was thirty-seven years to the day since the simultaneous deaths of Adams and Jefferson and four score and seven years to the day since the ratification of the Declaration of Independence.

THE FINAL DEAL

When you read of social or moral truths being self-evident or universally acknowledged, know that the writer either suffers severe self-delusion or is pulling your leg. The clergy's attempt to determine if God considered slavery a blessing was futile and irrelevant. They were examining the wrong issue. The founding fathers had pledged to form a government dedicated to the principle that God has granted everyone equal rights. Among these rights are life, liberty, and the pursuit of happiness. All the clergy needed to do was recognize that the founding fathers had made that pledge and ask themselves if people are obligated to keep pledges made to God.

Before the war, Methodist had been conflicted over the morality of Southern slavery. After the war, many Methodist leaders viewed the outcome of the war as evidence that God opposed slavery. "The course of the war was considered as conclusive proof that God had somehow led and guided the North and confounded the South."[25] "While northern Methodists proclaimed that the Civil War was being waged to preserve the Union, they also declared that the contest was God's chastisement visited upon the nation for permitting the evil of slavery to exist for almost a century after the Declaration of Independence had been issued."[26] Their logic was flawed. Other nations had practiced slavery with no apparent Divine judgment, but those nations had not pledged to form a government guaranteeing the right of liberty to all inhabitants. The Declaration pledge commissioned God to judge the United States for failure to comply with this founding principle.

After the war, the vast majority of Confederates did not consider their defeat as a judgment from God. Colonel William Oates, commander of Confederate forces assaulting Little Round Top, said, "God had nothing to do with it. He never diverted a bullet from one man, or caused it to hit another, nor directed who should fall or who should escape, nor how the battle should terminate."[27] Colonel Oates did not believe that God judged the wicked and rewarded the righteous in this life.

Historians to date have not connected the clear meaning of the Declaration's text with succeeding events. Nevertheless, the question of whether or not the Declaration is a covenant with God and the Civil War judgment for failing to comply begs an answer. There is a correct answer and it should inform and guide future decisions.

When thou vowest a vow unto God, defer not to pay it; for he hath no pleasure in fools: pay that which thou hast vowed
(ECCLESIASTES 5:4).

CHAPTER ELEVEN

TODAY'S APPLICATION

This know also, that in the last days perilous times shall come.

For men shall be lovers of their own selves, covetous, boasters, proud, blasphemers, disobedient to parents, unthankful, unholy,

Without natural affection, trucebreakers, false accusers, incontinent, fierce, despisers of those that are good,

Traitors, heady, highminded, lovers of pleasures more than lovers of God;

Having a form of godliness, but denying the power thereof: from such turn away.

For of this sort are they which creep into houses, and lead captive silly women laden with sins, led away with divers lusts,

Ever learning, and never able to come to the knowledge of the truth

(2 TIMOTHY 3:1–7).

f abolitionists were correct when referring to the Declaration of Independence, then those same arguments remain valid today. The covenant promise the colonies made to guarantee everyone's rights to life, liberty, and the pursuit of happiness is still binding. Just as God determines who is entitled to the right to liberty, God also determines who is entitled to the right to life. Unfortunately we live amongst a people who believe there are no moral consequences for denying the right to life for unborn babies. On November 25, 2015, FOX News reported on a pole in which two-percent of the polees chose abortion as the most important issue facing the nation. Based upon the nation's response to abortion, a candid world could reach no other conclusion than that today's citizens now believe the Declaration to be "'a diplomatic dodge;' adopted merely for the purpose of excusing the rebellious Colonies ... a hypocritical piece of special pleading, drawn up by a batch of artful pettifoggers...the most impudent imposition ever practiced upon the whole world!"[1] But how do they explain the simultaneous deaths of Adams and Jefferson, the two key Northern victories at Gettysburg and Vicksburg on the Fourth of July following the Emancipation Proclamation, and the language of the document itself? Will citizens continue to ignore the obvious meaning of the words in our founding document?

The issue of when life begins can be argued from a biblical or a biological perspective. The Bible implies that life begins at conception in the story of Samson.

Before Samson was conceived, an angel appeared to his mother announcing the event.

> **And the angel of the Lord appeared unto the woman, and said unto her, Behold now, thou art barren, and bearest not: but thou shalt conceive, and bear a son.**
>
> **Now therefore beware, I pray thee, and drink not wine nor strong drink, and eat not any unclean thing:**
>
> **For, lo, thou shalt conceive, and bear a son; and no razor shall come on his head: for the child shall be a Nazarite unto God from the womb**
> (JUDGES 13:3-5A).

Samson's mother was instructed to begin obeying Nazarite dietary restrictions before conception because her son would be a Nazarite to God from the womb. The mother did not follow the Nazarite diet because she was a Nazarite but because her son who was yet to be conceived would be a Nazarite. Beyond all contradictions, God only makes people Nazarites. He does not make a clump of cells a Nazarite. Samson was a person from the moment of conception and, therefore, eligible to be a Nazarite.

> **But he said unto me, Behold, thou shalt conceive, and bear a son; and now drink no wine nor strong drink, neither eat any unclean thing: for the child shall be a Nazarite to God from the womb to the day of his death.**

She may not eat of any thing that cometh of the vine, neither let her drink wine or strong drink, nor eat any unclean thing
(JUDGES 13:7, 14A).

Three times in the thirteenth chapter of Judges, the Bible uses the phrase, "conceive and bear." Samson's story would remain unchanged if God had said Samson was a Nazarite from birth. The dietary restrictions convey the truth that life begins at conception.

The Bible confirms that Jesus was conceived.

And, behold, thou shalt conceive in thy womb, and bring forth a son, and shalt call his name JESUS.

And when eight days were accomplished for the circumcising of the child, his name was called JESUS, which was so named of the angel before he was conceived in the womb
(LUKE 1:31, 2:21).

Fortunately for humanity, Mary did not choose to end an inconvenient pregnancy but chose instead to nurture the life within her.

The biological argument is equally clear. A fertilized egg begins cell division immediately after conception even before it implants in the womb. This is evidence of life. The truth that the unborn baby is human life is universally acknowledged as illustrated by the purchase of fetal tissue for human research. Nevertheless, we are infested by people who consider it acceptable to sell fetal tissue for research while refusing to acknowledge the unborn child as human.

Abortion advocates refuse to be drawn into a debate about when life begins. They know they will lose their point whenever this happens. They can point to no reasonable alternative to conception. They, therefore, refuse to consider the question while zealously defending their contrived right to murder the unborn. People who feel they can support abortion without first determining when life begins are unconcerned about moral consequences.

The country's last realistic chance to avoid moral consequences was the election of 2008. That election was an application of Deuteronomy 30:19.

> **I call heaven and earth to record this day against you, that I have set before you life and death, blessing and cursing: therefore choose life, that both thou and thy seed may live.**

Republican Vice-presidential candidate Sarah Palin had just given birth to a Down syndrome baby. Many couples with demanding jobs and grown children would have chosen to abort this baby. Ninety percent of Down syndrome babies are aborted.

By contrast, Barrack Obama was the most pro-abortion candidate to ever run for president. He voted four times to deprive medical care for babies surviving abortion. He co-sponsored the *Freedom of Choice Act,* which would have made partial-birth abortion legal again and force taxpayers to pay for abortions. One of his leading qualifications in a running mate was that he also be pro-abortion. Joe Biden said, "I strongly support *Roe v. Wade*. . . That's why I led the fight to defeat Bork. Thank God he is not in the Court or *Roe v Wade* would be gone by now."

Despite this clear choice, most voters considered the economy more important than moral issues and, in so doing, voted to continue murdering unborn children. It is not possible to choose death for unborn children and life and blessing for ourselves. Those who voted for Obama chose death and cursing for themselves, their families, and this nation. A significant number of citizens failed to vote. These also chose death for God did not instruct us to avoid choosing death but to choose life which they refused to do. Consider the wisdom and justice of God. Those who nonchalantly voted judgment on the nation simultaneously voted judgment on themselves. When they get what they chose, they blame others. Mankind's refusal to accept responsibility is a consistent characteristic of human nature demonstrated clearly by the refusal of Confederates to admit God judged them over their continued defense of slavery. Just as Confederates continued to proclaim their righteousness, abortion advocates re-elected Obama. The brutality of slavery deterred Confederates from admitting they fought a war to defend it. The horrific nature of abortion makes it difficult for people to change their minds on this issue and admit they supported the murder of 60,000,000 unborn babies. The country cannot escape judgment, but individuals can avoid it by defending innocent life.

Judgment of the nation began with the election of Barack Obama. The same people who thought they could support abortion without first considering when life begins, elected Obama without first resolving his legal status. Those who believe there are no moral consequences for murdering unborn babies will believe anything. Obama posted a fraudulent birth certificate on the White House web site and released a fraudulent selective service registration form.[2] He is using a fraudulent social security number.[3] Anyone else caught in these deceptions would logically be considered an illegal alien. Consistency demands the same conclusion for Obama.

Ignorant of our history, we have repeated the sins of the past. Confederates broke the Declaration covenant by failing to protect everyone's liberty. Today's citizens ignore both founding documents, breaking the Declaration covenant by failing to protect everyone's life while shredding the constitutional requirement for the president to be a natural born citizen.

There are Christians who believe they can vote for abortion candidates and remain in God's favor just as there were Christians who thought they could support slavery and remain in God's favor. Both are deceived. When Planned Parenthood began, it advocated birth control arguing that it prevented the murder of unborn children through abortion. Now it promotes murder while convincing women that those protecting unborn children are waging war against them. These women permit the sale of the body parts from their unborn children to be used in human research but refuse to acknowledge the humanity of these babies. They think they have a right to murder their unborn children, a right offered by Satan in his kingdom.

No group has so consistently violated the covenant as blacks. They protest that they are men and women claiming their Declaration rights while denying them to unborn babies. They attribute their circumstances to white privilege. Consider an alternative paradigm. God defends the weak and defenseless. The same God who grieved over the institution of slavery mourns the murder of unborn babies. He cannot bless those who choose death and cursing.

Many think the economy is the most important political issue. Consider an alternative paradigm. Recall the covenant our founding fathers initiated acknowledging everyone's right to life. Consider God's judgment upon a nation abrogating its responsibilities to unborn children and ask yourselves how such a nation can thrive.

Hispanics think they can punish politicians who will not grant citizen status to those who entered the country illegally. Consider an alternative paradigm. Citizens of this country are constrained by a covenant with God. Failure to comply with that covenant brings divine judgment first of all on the country and secondly on all those who contribute to this failure. Those who seek a country where they can decide on the nation's course without divine judgment, must look elsewhere.

Silly women led captive by Planned Parenthood theology believe they can break the sacred bond between mother and unborn child without moral repercussions. Consider an alternative paradigm.

**Be not deceived; God is not mocked: for
whatsoever a man soweth, that shall he also reap**
(GALATIANS 6:7).

Some think the greatest threat to this country is from
radical Islam, Russia, or China. Consider an alternative
paradigm. This country could not be defeated while
it had God's blessing. Having broken the covenant,
this country can only anticipate judgment and fiery
indignation as we are devoured by our adversaries. Our
most lethal enemies were within convincing the gullible
and Supreme Court justices that unborn children
were not people in the eyes of God. If the judgment
for slavery was 620,000 deaths, the maiming of many
more, the destruction of Southern infrastructure and
economy, what will the judgment be for government
sanctioned murder of 60,000,000 unborn babies?

Satan is never satisfied with a cadre of fools
implementing his evil schemes. During the slavery
debate, he instigated a scheme to involve those opposed
to slavery with the *Fugitive Slave Act*. Failure to assist in
capturing escaped slaves exposed people to stiff penalties.
Today, Satan's minions seek to involve pro-life citizens
by demanding that government funds fund abortion.

Extensive moral blindness is not unique to this
generation. The Confederacy was similarly afflicted.
The nation of Israel exhibited this characteristic in
Bible times.

**Run ye to and fro through the streets of
Jerusalem, and see now, and know, and seek in**

**the broad places thereof, if ye can find a man,
if there be any that executeth judgment, that
seeketh the truth; and I will pardon it.**

**And though they say, The Lord liveth; surely
they swear falsely.**

**O Lord, are not thine eyes upon the truth? thou
hast stricken them, but they have not grieved;
thou hast consumed them, but they have refused
to receive correction: they have made their faces
harder than a rock; they have refused to return.**

**Therefore I said, Surely these are poor; they are
foolish: for they know not the way of the Lord,
nor the judgment of their God**

(JEREMIAH 5:1-4).

Citizens elected an illegal alien who promised to
fundamentally change the nation without determining
the changes he advocated. The country has been in steep
decline since. This has been a judgment from God which
citizens of this country have refused to acknowledge.
They blame elected officials for the continued decline
of the country while they should be judging themselves
for repeatedly electing a sufficient number of officials to
defend, promote, and pay for the continued murder of
unborn children.

**their everlasting confusion shall never be
forgotten**

(JEREMIAH 20:11B).

237

The constitution acknowledged the existence of slavery and implicitly condoned it. Nowhere does it condone the murder of unborn babies.

Make your home on the shores of Puget Sound and expect that it will not be swept away by an offshore generated tidal wave, but do not think that a nation can ignore its covenant with God with government sanctioned murder of 60,000,000 unborn babies and successfully solicit divine favor. Satan successfully brought judgment on this nation once for violating our covenant to protect mankind's liberty. He has successfully brought judgment on it once again for failing to protect the right of life for the most vulnerable. It is another terrifying example of what he is capable of accomplishing through his own line.

YOUNG THEODORE

Little Theodore sleeps in his warm habitation where danger should never intrude.

Where new babes rest securely in safe sequestration in silence of black solitude.

As a gift from the Father, he's always well nourished, each day only good he'd consume.

As a blessing from God his creator, he flourished while nestled in Mommy's snug womb.

Where mom's love as a blanket provided protection as evils were lurking outside

It was nature's appointment by holy selection in mommies this charge to confide

That such bounty bestowed was so grudgingly given young Theodore stayed unaware.

This poor babe since Mom's acts by self-interest were driven would never be tasting fresh air.

Accidently conceived he had no revelation that he and his mom were in strife.

In the womb he received mommy's just allocation of everything needed for life.

Naïve Theodore trusted without reservation expecting sweet calm to remain

While his mommy was plotting discrete separation her freedom and plans to retain.

Where the baby resided, God's blessing provided protection God's laws to obey.

Unbeknownst to young Theodore, courts had decided his mommy should have the last say.

While his mommy was plotting intentions pernicious employing her freedom of choice,

Little Theodore slept and remained unsuspicious of plans where he hadn't a voice.

While young Theodore nestled in blissful delusion, his mommy had plotted his harm

As sharp scissors presented a vicious intrusion commencing to severe his arm.

In his heart there arose an unshaken conviction that mommies their children protect.

Since he couldn't conceive a conflicting depiction, all doubts of his mom he'd reject.

The commissioned grim reaper by God's chosen keeper was causing young Theodore stress.

As his mommy was choosing the choice that was cheaper, what thoughts would her baby express?

He would gaze on Mom's face as he sought her affection each line he would carefully trace.

In the hope he'd encounter a strengthened connection, one handed he'd seek her embrace.

But the babe was still clutching his cherished delusion that Mommy was always his friend.

He considered no logic against this conclusion. No other could he comprehend.

Life's provider was good, though he couldn't explain it, he trusted with all of his heart

Thus his arm must be bad so he shouldn't retain it rejoicing that it must depart.

He was forced to admit that the cruel amputation accompanied eye-popping pain,

But that useless appendage deserved mutilation while losing its right to remain.

While perceiving the scissor's returning intrusion, he felt no compulsion to beg,

So imagine young Theodore's instant confusion when scissors start gnawing his leg.

That no evil would ever gain Mommy's permission young Theodore staunchly believed

So he couldn't explain how the scissors admission so viciously vile was achieved.

To the truth of his mommy's most cruel invitation young Theodore couldn't adjust.

Such absurd rumination defied contemplation.
In Mom he'd continue to trust.

Now the evil continues, most vile penetration,
which Theodore wished he could check

With his trust in his mom as his sole consolation
the scissors start sawing his neck.

From the day of conception from mommy's
compassion each token of life was obtained.

It was only such generous bounty could fashion
unbroken a bond still unstrained.

Not vexatious by nature, this mommy rejection
a thought he could not understand.

Still audacious in hope of his mommy's affection,
he sought her compassionate hand.

With his life on the ebb and without arbitrator
his vicious attack to protest,

And not knowing the source of the grim
perpetrator, he gurgled his final request.

With all else stripped away, he continued
audacious one hope he decided to clutch

And unable to think of his mom as ungracious
he sought her affectionate touch.

Twould mean so much.

No memorial humble was ever erected for Theodore's bodily parts

For most people prefer to forget the rejected when actions expose evil hearts.

No grand sights would he see while great thoughts contemplating. In sports he would never compete.

No loud cheers reached his ears from wild throngs celebrating his latest spectacular feat.

And did Mommy remember affection forsaken when plotting her baby to slay?

She avoided reflecting on actions she'd taken on that unforgettable day.

With her faith in a deity's favor unshaken true virtue to surely repay

In her heart she still cherished the hope she'd awaken to husband and children one day.

Obama is not our problem. Our problem is that 98% of the population think they can determine what is moral. They think they can ignore abortion. Judgment is coming. It will look like the whole nation is being judged because judgment is coming upon 98% of the population.

CHAPTER TWELVE

KNOWING THE TIME

Jesus and the epistles tell us that we should know the times. As God's tribulation judgment approaches, we should not be taken by surprise.

> **He answered and said unto them, When it is evening, ye say, It will be fair weather: for the sky is red.**
>
> **And in the morning, It will be foul weather to day: for the sky is red and lowring. O ye hypocrites, ye can discern the face of the sky; but can ye not discern the signs of the times?**
>
> (MATTHEW 16:2–3)

> **And that, knowing the time, that now it is high time to awake out of sleep: for now is our salvation nearer than when we believed**
>
> (ROMANS 13:11).

> **For yourselves know perfectly that the day of the Lord so cometh as a thief in the night.**

For when they shall say, Peace and safety; then sudden destruction cometh upon them, as travail upon a woman with child; and they shall not escape.

But ye, brethren, are not in darkness, that that day should overtake you as a thief
(1 THESSALONIANS 5:2–4).

The prophesied tribulation is at hand. The Bible gives us signs that point to specific dates. Daniel's seventy week prophecy tells us there will be a seven-year tribulation period and enables us to determine when it will begin.

Seventy weeks are determined upon thy people and upon thy holy city, to finish the transgression, and to make an end of sins, and to make reconciliation for iniquity, and to bring in everlasting righteousness, and to seal up the vision and prophecy, and to anoint the most Holy.

Know therefore and understand, that from the going forth of the commandment to restore and to build Jerusalem unto the Messiah the Prince shall be seven weeks, and threescore and two weeks: the street shall be built again, and the wall, even in troublous times.

And after threescore and two weeks shall Messiah be cut off, but not for himself: and the people of the prince that shall come shall destroy the city and the sanctuary; and the end

thereof shall be with a flood, and unto the end of the war desolations are determined.

And he shall confirm the covenant with many for one week: and in the midst of the week he shall cause the sacrifice and the oblation to cease, and for the overspreading of abominations he shall make it desolate, even until the consummation, and that determined shall be poured upon the desolate
(DANIEL 9:24–27).

At the time of Daniel's prophecy, both the Jews and Jerusalem existed. God told Daniel, the prophesied time would begin when the Jews were commanded to rebuild Jerusalem. The seventy weeks apply just as much to Jerusalem as to the Jews: "**Seventy weeks are determined upon thy people and upon thy holy city.**"

God divided the 70 weeks into three groups: 7 + 62 + 1 = 70. Each week represents seven years for a total of 490 years. The first two groups, 7 and 62, occurred in sequence. When the commandment was given to rebuild Jerusalem, the 69 weeks, 483 years, commenced. After 483 years, Jesus was crucified and the time of the prophecy stopped. The remaining week coincides with a seven year treaty between the Jews and the Antichrist.

The text gives no explanation for dividing the first 69 weeks into 7 and 62. The fact that God separated the first 7 weeks is significant. Just as the 7 weeks preceded the 62 weeks, it will also precede the last week. In other words, the clock is not waiting for the Antichrist covenant with Israel to start ticking. It started ticking again when the Jews gained control of Jerusalem. Israel gained control over Jerusalem in the Six-Day War fought in 1967. If we add 49 (seven weeks) to 1967, we get 2016.

The Jews gained control of Jerusalem on June 7, 1967. So the tribulation should start 49 years from that day. Using the Gregorian calendar, this would be June 7, 2016. However, it is possible that God may not use the Gregorian calendar. The pure definition of a year is one revolution of the earth about the sun. It takes approximately 356.25 days for the earth to revolve about the sun. The Gregorian calendar adjusts for the partial day by adding one day every leap year. In 49 years we would need to add 12 and one quarter days. In the interval of interest there are 13 leap days starting in 1968 with the last one being in 2016. Therefore, a more accurate representation of the revolution of the earth about the sun would include only 12 leap days. If we take out the leap day for 2016, the day we currently label June 7 would become June 8. Therefore, June 8 is the most likely day for the signing of the seven-year peace treaty. The Jewish calendar offers another alternative, which is based on the revolution of the moon around the earth with each revolution representing a Jewish month. In the Jewish calendar, June 7, 1967 is the 28 of Iyyar, 5727.[1] The 28 of Iyyar, 5776 becomes June 5, 2016.

According to the Daniel prophesy, the Antichrist will sign a seven year treaty with the Jews to mark the beginning of the tribulation. This will probably occur on June 8 but could occur on June 5 or 7. If Israel does not sign a seven-year peace treaty by the 10, disregard everything I have written. Burn this book. If friends have a copy, tell them to burn it.

The seventy weeks in Daniel 9 "**are determined upon thy people**," the Jews. In order for the seven weeks to precede the one week tribulation, it must be a time of the Jews. However, the Bible says that when Jerusalem was taken by the Jews, the times of the Gentiles ended. When the Jews gained control of Jerusalem, it became, once again, a time of the Jews.

> **Jerusalem shall be trodden down of the Gentiles, until the times of the Gentiles be fulfilled**
> (LUKE 21:24B).

We always knew the tribulation was a time of the Jews being called a time of Jacob's troubles.

> **Alas! for that day is great, so that none is like it: it is even the time of Jacob's trouble; but he shall be saved out of it**
> (JEREMIAH 30:7).

However, we have been living in the time of the Jews ever since June of 1967.

Jerusalem is not the only location of significance in prophesy. The prophecy in Mark 13:28–30 refers to the nation of Israel.

> **Now learn a parable of the fig tree; When her branch is yet tender, and putteth forth leaves, ye know that summer is near:**

So ye in like manner, when ye shall see these things come to pass, know that it is nigh, even at the doors.

Verily I say unto you, that this generation shall not pass, till all these things be done
(MARK 13:28–30).

The fig tree represents Israel, and we saw the fig tree putting forth leaves when the nation of Israel was founded in 1948. So when would that generation pass away? Although the tribulation starts in 2016, that is not when all things will be done. All things will not be done until the tribulation ends seven years later in 2023. That would be 75 years after the formation of the nation of Israel (2023– 1948). I was alive in 1948 having been born in 1946, but I was not aware of the nation of Israel being formed. Am I a member of the generation that saw the fig tree putting forth leaves? I think not.

The Bible talks about generations in the book of Numbers.

And the LORD's anger was kindled against Israel, and he made them wander in the wilderness forty years, until all the generation, that had done evil in the sight of the LORD, was consumed
(NUMBERS 32:13).

The generation spoken of in Numbers included everyone who was twenty years or older.

> **Your carcases shall fall in this wilderness; and all that were numbered of you, according to your whole number, from twenty years old and upward, which have murmured against me**
> (NUMBERS 14:29).

Applying the twenty year rule to the prophecy in Mark, we see that everyone in the generation that saw the fig tree putting forth leaves must be 95 or older in June of 2023. There would be few people of that age who survived the tribulation.

The prophet Joel describes signs in the heavens for the coming tribulation.

> **The sun shall be turned into darkness, and the moon into blood, before the great and the terrible day of the LORD come**
> (JOEL 2:31).

We have just experienced fulfillment of this sign in the form of lunar and solar eclipses. During a lunar eclipse, the moon passes through the earth's shadow. When this occurs, the moon turns red due to the refraction of the sun's rays passing through the earth's atmosphere. As the rays pass through the atmosphere, the red rays are bent and hit the moon giving it a reddish color. We have just completed a blood moon tetrad, four consecutive full lunar eclipses without an intervening partial lunar eclipse. These lunar eclipses occurred on Jewish feast days, Unleavened Bread 2014 and 2015 and Tabernacles 2014 and 2015. In addition, a full solar eclipse occurred on March 20, 2015 which was Nisan 1, the beginning of the year on the Jewish calendar.[2]

There will not be another tetrad falling on the Jewish feast days in this century. We will not have time to experience another tetrad before all the generation which saw the fig tree putting forth leaves has passed away. The one we just experienced must be the one that is prophesied. Notice that the Joel prophecy says that this must happen before the day of the Lord. The tetrad must be completed along with the solar eclipse before the day of the Lord, tribulation, begins. The tetrad ended in September, 2015. The tribulation will begin in June 2016, less than a year later.

The tetrad we just experienced is the ninth tetrad since Jesus with all the lunar eclipses falling on the Jewish feast days of Unleavened Bread and Tabernacles. The number nine is significant in scripture. "It is the last of the digits, and thus marks the end; and is significant of the conclusion of a matter.

It is akin to the number six, six being the sum of its factors (3 x 3 = 9, and 3 + 3 = 6), and is thus significant of the end of man, and the summation of all man's works. Nine is, therefore, THE NUMBER OF FINALITY OR JUDGMENT. . ."[3]

Another event that will occur during this time period is the catching away of the church known as the rapture. Paul described the rapture in his first letter to the Thessalonians.

For this we say unto you by the word of the Lord, that we which are alive and remain unto the coming of the Lord shall not prevent them which are asleep.

> For the Lord himself shall descend from heaven
> with a shout, with the voice of the archangel,
> and with the trump of God: and the dead in
> Christ shall rise first:
>
> Then we which are alive and remain shall be
> caught up together with them in the clouds, to
> meet the Lord in the air: and so shall we ever be
> with the Lord
>
> (1 THESSALONIANS 4:15–17).

At least some of the Thessalonians became worried that the rapture had already occurred, and they had been left behind.

> Now we beseech you, brethren, by the coming
> of our Lord Jesus Christ, and by our gathering
> together unto him,
>
> That ye be not soon shaken in mind, or be
> troubled, neither by spirit, nor by word, nor by
> letter as from us, as that the day of Christ is at
> hand.
>
> Let no man deceive you by any means: for that
> day shall not come, except there come a falling
> away first, and that man of sin be revealed, the
> son of perdition;
>
> Who opposeth and exalteth himself above all
> that is called God, or that is worshipped; so that
> he as God sitteth in the temple of God, shewing
> himself that he is God
>
> (2 THESSALONIANS 2:1–4).

Paul said the rapture, called the "day of Christ," will not happen until the Antichrist is revealed. The specific sign given is that the Antichrist will be in the temple of God, showing himself that he is God. The rapture cannot happen before this sign which occurs according to Daniel 9:27 midway through the tribulation.

We are about to enter into the time period that concerned the Thessalonians. The church must go through the first half of the tribulation. Jesus told a parable confirming that the church will not be pulled out too early while confirming that at least part of the church will be strong and mature.

But while men slept, his enemy came and sowed tares among the wheat, and went his way.

But when the blade was sprung up, and brought forth fruit, then appeared the tares also.

So the servants of the householder came and said unto him, Sir, didst not thou sow good seed in thy field? from whence then hath it tares?

He said unto them, An enemy hath done this. The servants said unto him, Wilt thou then that we go and gather them up?

But he said, Nay; lest while ye gather up the tares, ye root up also the wheat with them.

Let both grow together until the harvest: and in the time of harvest I will say to the reapers,

> Gather ye together first the tares, and bind them
> in bundles to burn them: but gather the wheat
> into my barn
>
> (MATTHEW 13:25–30).

Jesus said both would grow together. It will be the power of Satan verses the power of God. God is well able to equip his church to confront the powers of darkness.

The later chapters in Isaiah prophesy that there will be a glorious church during the tribulation period.

> Arise, shine; for thy light is come, and the glory
> of the LORD is risen upon thee.
>
> For, behold, the darkness shall cover the earth,
> and gross darkness the people: but the LORD
> shall arise upon thee, and his glory shall be seen
> upon thee
>
> (ISAIAH 60:1, 2).

The tribulation is less than a year away. This prophecy must be fulfilled. The glory of the Lord will rise upon his people during a period of gross darkness. There will be no period of gross darkness following the tribulation during the millennial reign of Jesus. This prophecy must be fulfilled during the tribulation. Many view the rapture as God's evacuation plan to rescue the church as Satan and his minions storm the gates. This is not the picture in scripture. Satan hides for the first half of the tribulation in fear of the overcoming church.

And the God of peace shall bruise Satan under your feet shortly

(ROMANS 16:20A).

The description of the glorious church continues in Isaiah, chapter 61.

The Spirit of the Lord GOD is upon me; because the LORD hath anointed me to preach good tidings unto the meek; he hath sent me to bind up the brokenhearted, to proclaim liberty to the captives, and the opening of the prison to them that are bound;

To proclaim the acceptable year of the LORD, and the day of vengeance of our God; to comfort all that mourn;

To appoint unto them that mourn in Zion, to give unto them beauty for ashes, the oil of joy for mourning, the garment of praise for the spirit of heaviness; that they might be called trees of righteousness, the planting of the LORD, that he might be glorified.

And they shall build the old wastes, they shall raise up the former desolations, and they shall repair the waste cities, the desolations of many generations.

And strangers shall stand and feed your flocks, and the sons of the alien shall be your plowmen and your vinedressers.

But ye shall be named the Priests of the LORD: men shall call you the Ministers of our God: ye shall eat the riches of the Gentiles, and in their glory shall ye boast yourselves

(ISAIAH 61:1–6).

Jesus quoted verse one and part of verse two to explain his earthly ministry (Luke 4:18, 19). The remainder of that ministry is about to be fulfilled. While God is judging the world, those in Zion walk in great power. We know Zion can refer to the New Covenant because Hebrews tells us that we have come to Mount Zion (Hebrews 12:22). This verse tells us those in Zion will be named priests and ministers to God. Under the Old Covenant, only the descendants of Aaron were called to be priests. Under the New Covenant, all Christians are called to be priests (Revelation 1:6,5:10).

The Christian church becomes glorious by beholding the glory of Jesus.

But we all, with open face beholding as in a glass the glory of the Lord, are changed into the same image from glory to glory, even as by the Spirit of the Lord.

(2 CORINTHIANS 3:18).

The context of this verse plainly states that no one under the Old Covenant can behold this glory.

God will reveal the glory of Jesus to us through the Holy Spirit.

Howbeit when he, the Spirit of truth, is come, he will guide you into all truth: for he shall not

speak of himself; but whatsoever he shall hear, that shall he speak: and he will shew you things to come.

He shall glorify me: for he shall receive of mine, and shall shew it unto you
(JOHN 16:13–14).

There will be an outpouring of the Holy Spirit during this time to reveal the glory of Jesus. This will rapidly mature those who look for this outpouring enabling them to walk in the prophesied glory.

Scripture prophesies this outpouring calling it several names. It is called the former and latter rain.

Be patient therefore, brethren, unto the coming of the Lord. Behold, the husbandman waiteth for the precious fruit of the earth, and hath long patience for it, until he receive the early and latter rain
(JAMES 5:7).

The prophesied event that will raise up the glorious church is called the glorious appearing.

Looking for that blessed hope, and the glorious appearing of the great God and our Saviour Jesus Christ;

Who gave himself for us, that he might redeem us from all iniquity, and purify unto himself a peculiar people, zealous of good works
(TITUS 2:13-14).

It is referred to as David's tabernacle.

In that day will I raise up the tabernacle of David that is fallen, and close up the breaches thereof; and I will raise up his ruins, and I will build it as in the days of old

(AMOS 9:11).

The word "Zion" is key to this study.

Thou shalt arise, and have mercy upon Zion: for the time to favour her, yea, the set time, is come.

For thy servants take pleasure in her stones, and favour the dust thereof.

So the heathen shall fear the name of the Lord, and all the kings of the earth thy glory.

When the Lord shall build up Zion, he shall appear in his glory

(PSALM 102:13–16).

This passage confirms that there is a set time in which this outpouring of the Holy Spirit called the "glorious appearing" will occur. The set time to favor Zion corresponds to the glorious appearing. God favors Zion through the glorious appearing.

Zion is also connected with the former and latter rain which represents the outpouring of the Holy Spirit during this time.

Be glad then, ye children of Zion, and rejoice in the LORD your God: for he hath given you the former rain moderately, and he will cause to come down for you the rain, the former rain, and the latter rain in the first month

(JOEL 2:23).

The glory will be experienced by the church at the beginning of the tribulation. The word "month" is in italics, meaning it was added at the discretion of the translator. Nevertheless, the meaning is clear. The outpouring of the Holy Spirit occurs at the beginning of the tribulation.

Not only does Scripture tell us that there is a set time for God to favor Zion, but it also says there is a time for the former and latter rain.

Ask ye of the Lord rain in the time of the latter rain

(ZECHARIAH 10:1A).

The prophecies about the glorious appearing, the time to favor Zion, the outpouring of the former and latter rains, and the time of David's tabernacle must all take place before the millennial reign of Jesus.

What should we do now that the tribulation is almost upon us? Most Christians will not experience the glorious appearing and become a part of the overcoming church.

So Christ was once offered to bear the sins of many; and unto them that look for him shall

he appear the second time without sin unto salvation
(HEBREWS 9:28).

By saying he will appear to those who "**look for him**," scripture implies that Jesus will not appear to those who are not looking for him. Many think they are obeying this admonition by studying end time signs and expecting to be raptured. That is not the attitude this scripture describes. Scripture does not say Jesus will appear to those who are "looking for the second coming" but to those who "**look for him**." By saying we should "**look for him**" the scripture is describing those Christians who are seeking to experience the presence of the Lord because of their love for him.

For the eyes of the LORD run to and fro throughout the whole earth, to shew himself strong in the behalf of them whose heart is perfect toward him
(2 CHRONICLES 16:9A).

but the people that do know their God shall be strong, and do exploits
(DANIEL 11:32B).

Those who want to be a part of the overcoming church must actively seek the presence of the Lord.

God will not rapture the whole Christian church. Jesus is not anxious to be with those who are lukewarm.

So then because thou art lukewarm, and neither cold nor hot, I will spue thee out of my mouth
(REVELATION 3:16).

The rapture occurs to remove the overcoming church so that the fruits of iniquity can fully manifest and be understood.

For the mystery of iniquity doth already work: only he who now letteth will let, until he be taken out of the way
(2 THESSALONIANS 2:7).

The Holy Spirit in the glorious church will be taken out of the way in the rapture. Those who are not passionately seeking the Lord's presence will not be a part of the overcoming church and will not be raptured. Those who vote for abortion candidates, or think the economy is the overriding issue of the day, or cannot be bothered to vote to save the lives of unborn children should stock up on seven years of tribulation food.

Since Jesus was crucified on Passover, rose on First Fruits, and the Holy Spirit came on Pentecost, many look for him to come on one of the important days during the fall. These days would include Rosh Hashanah, the Day of Atonement or Yom Kippur, and the feast of Tabernacles. Neither the rapture nor the return of Jesus lines up with these days.

The Feast of Tabernacles celebrates God dwelling among his people. The presence of Jesus abides with us during the first half of the tribulation to change us from glory to glory into his image. The possible timing lines up most closely with this event. One of the terms the Bible uses to describe this time is David's tabernacle.

> **After this I will return, and will build again the tabernacle of David, which is fallen down; and I will build again the ruins thereof, and I will set it up:**
>
> **That the residue of men might seek after the Lord, and all the Gentiles, upon whom my name is called, saith the Lord, who doeth all these things**
> (ACTS 15:16–17).

The concept of Jesus "returning" refers more to the restoration of David's tabernacle than to Jesus coming at the end of the tribulation.

The fall feast days reveal something important for each of these imminent events. The Day of Atonement precedes the Feast illustrating man's need for repentance and cleansing prior to encountering God. God sent John the Baptist to prepare the way for the ministry of Jesus (Matthew 3:3). The ministry of John the Baptist was prophesied in the book of Isaiah.

> **The voice of him that crieth in the wilderness, Prepare ye the way of the Lord, make straight in the desert a highway for our God.**
>
> **Every valley shall be exalted, and every mountain and hill shall be made low: and the crooked shall be made straight, and the rough places plain:**

And the glory of the Lord shall be revealed, and all flesh shall see it together: for the mouth of the Lord hath spoken it
(ISAIAH 40:3–5).

At that time, the glory of the Lord appeared in the physical body of Jesus. We are about the experience the glory of the Lord as the Holy Spirit reveals the presence of Jesus. We need to prepare for the glorious appearing of Jesus which should include repentance of any sins the Holy Spirit brings to mind. The reluctance to repent was clearly illustrated by Confederates' reluctance to admit they fought the war over slavery. Repentance is certainly required for all who have failed to oppose abortion. Nobody dropped dead because of sins when in the presence of Jesus, but Ananias and Sapphira died when they lied to the Holy Spirit. Those seeking the presence of Jesus cannot afford to be deluded about their righteousness.

The Bible also prophecies of a battle which must take place before the millennial reign of Jesus called the battle of Gog and Magog (Ezekiel 38, 39). A great army comes against Israel and destroys itself. Israel will take seven years to burn the debris from this battle. It is more likely that Israel will have cleared the debris before the start of the millennial reign of Jesus which would put the start of the battle sometime before the beginning of the tribulation.

Why have we not been warned about the start of the tribulation? Scripture reveals that many of those we call watchmen will be asleep.

For thus hath the Lord said unto me, Go, set a watchman, let him declare what he seeth.

The burden of Dumah. He calleth to me out of Seir, Watchman, what of the night? Watchman, what of the night?

The watchman said, The morning cometh, and also the night.

(ISAIAH 21:6, 11–12A)

His watchmen are blind: they are all ignorant, they are all dumb dogs, they cannot bark; sleeping, lying down, loving to slumber.

Yea, they are greedy dogs which can never have enough, and they are shepherds that cannot understand: they all look to their own way, every one for his gain, from his quarter.

Come ye, say they, I will fetch wine, and we will fill ourselves with strong drink; and to morrow shall be as this day, and much more abundant

(ISAIAH 56:10–12).

Many of our paid watchmen tell us that morning follows night and night will follow morning. They tell us that tomorrow will be the same as yesterday. They have failed us. This much of what the watchmen are telling us is certainly true—night is coming, and it is imminent.

ENDNOTES

FOREWORD

1 Maier, Pauline, *American Scripture: Making of the Declaration of Independence*, Alfred A. Knopf, New York, 1997.

2 Maier, p 165.

3 Maier, p 136.

4 Jefferson, Thomas *Notes on the State of Virginia*, ed. William Peden. Chapel Hill, N.C.: University of North Carolina Press, 1955, p 163.

5 Maier, p xix.

6 Speech given by Carl Schurz at Springfield, Mass., quoted in *Daily Dispatch*, Richmond, Va., April 10, 1861, available at chroniclingamerica. loc.gov.

CHAPTER ONE

1 McCullough, David, *John Adams*, Simon & Schuster, New York, 2001, p 109.

2 McCullough, p 110.

3   McCullough, p 118.

4   McCullough, 135.

5   Social Security Actuarial Life Table for 2007, http://www.ssa.gov/oact/ STATS/table4c6.html.

6   McCullough, p 648.

7   Bible verses copied on Biblesoft software, version 2.1, Seattle, Wa, King James Version.

8   Fellman, Michael, Lesley J. Gordon, Daniel E Sutherland, *This Terrible War*, Pearson Education, Inc, 2008, p 416.

9   Howe, Julia Ward. *Reminiscences: 1819-1899*, Houghton, Mifflin: New York, 1899. p. 274.

10 Howe, p. 275.

CHAPTER TWO

1   The phrase, "the United States are," demonstrated that the predominant view of the nation was of a collection of independent states. People did not start using the phrase, "the United States is," until after the Civil War.

2   John Heywood, 1546, quoted on http://www.funtrivia.com/askft/ Question41522.html accessed 2/25/2016.

CHAPTER FOUR

1 Mayer Henry, *All on Fire, William Lloyd Garrison and the Abolition of Slavery*, W.W. Norton & Company, New York, London, p 53.

2 Mayer, p 176.

3 In a speech "No Compromise with Slavery," http://archive.org/stream/ nocompromisewith24194gut/ pg24194.txt accessed 2/25/2016.

4 Garrison, William Lloyd, Declaration of Sentiments of the American Anti-Slavery Society, 1833, http://utc.iath. virginia.edu/abolitn/abeswlgct.html accessed 2/25/2016.

5 Steiner, Bernard Christian, *Life of Roger Brooke Taney*, Williams & Wilkins Company, Baltimore, 1922, p 73.

6 Steiner, pp 75, 76.

7 Speech at Independence Hall by Abraham Lincoln on February 22, 1861, Philadelphia, Pennsylvania, quoted at http://teachingamericanhistory.org/ library/index.asp?documentprint=154, accessed 2/25/2016.

8 Eugene D. Genovese and Elizabeth Fox-Genovese, in *Looking South, Chapters in the Story of an American Region*, Edited by Winfred B. Moore, Jr. and Joseph R. Tripp, Greenwood Press, New York,

Westport Connecticut, London, 1989, p 35.

9 Genovese, pp 36, 37.

10 Ericson, David F., *The Debate over Slavery, Antislavery and Proslavery Liberalism in Antebellum America*, New York University Press, New York and London, p 20.

11 Ruffin, Edmund, in an article titled "African Colonization Unveiled," Richmond, P.D. Bernard printer 1853, p 2.

12 Hammond, James Henry, *Letter to an English Abolitinist*, 1845, quoted in *The Ideology of Slavery Proslavery thought in the Antebellum South, 1830-1860*, Ed. Drew Gilpin Faust, Baton Rouge, LA: Louisiana Stae UP, 1981, p 176.

13 John Quincy Adams Journal, www.masshist.org/jqadiaries/index.cfm, accessed 2/25/2016.

14 John C. Calhoun, http://www.constitution.org/jcc/disq_gov.txt, accessed 2/25/2016.

15 *The Gentleman's Magazine*, vol. 46, pp. 403-404.

16 Miller, William Lee, *Arguing about Slavery*, Alfred A. Knopf, New York, 1996, p 351.

CHAPTER FIVE

1 For a similar rationale, see Osterweis, Rollin G., *Romanticism and Nationalism in the Old South*, Yale University Press, New Haven, 1949, p 14.

2 Takaki, Ronald T., *A pro-slavery Crusade, The Agitation to Reopen the African Slave Trade*, Free Press, New York, New York, 1971, p 18.

3 *"The Causes of the American Civil War,"* Edited by Edwin C. Rozwenc, D.C. Heath and Company, 1961, p 1.

4 Rozwenc, Edwin C., *The Causes of the American Civil War*, D.C. Heath and Company, Boston, Ma, 1961, p 9.

5 *Richmond Enquirer*, March 13, quoted in Lorman A. Ratner and Dwight L. Teeter Jr., *Fanatics and Fire-eaters, Newspapers and the Coming of the Civil War*, University of Illinois Press, Urbana and Chicago, 2003, p 58.

6 Jefferson Davis, before a special session of the Confederate Congress, April 29, 1861, as quoted in *The Causes of the American Civil War*, Edited by Edwin C. Rozwenc, D.C. Heath and Company, 1961, p 31.

7 Robert Catlett Cave, a Saint Louis pastor speaking in Richmond in 1894, quoted in *The Myth of the Lost Cause and Civil War History*, Gary W.

Gallagher and Alan T. Nolan, editors, Indiana University Press, Bloomington and Indianapolis, 2000, p 206.

8 Chesebrough, David B., *Clergy Dissent in the Old South, 1830-1865*, Board of Trustees, Southern Illinois University, 1996, p 33.

9 Chesebrough, p 34.

10 *American Slavery as it is: Testimony of a Thousand Witnesses,* Assembled by Reverend Theodore Dwight Weld and Angelina and Sarah Grimke, New York, American Anti-Slavery Society, 1839, (available at docsouth.unc.edu), pp 194, 195.

11 Weld, p 198.

12 Weld, pp 188-190.

13 Extract from correspondence, Weld, p 207.

14 Mrs. D. Geraud Wright, "A Southern Girl in '61," pp. 31-32, quoted in Osterweis, Rollin G., *Romanticism and Nationalism in the Old South*, Yale University Press, New Haven, 1949, p 129.

15 Quoted in Miller, William Lee, *Arguing about Slavery*, Alfred A. Knopf, New York, 1996, p 340.

16 Quoted in Stowe, Harriet Beecher, *The Key to Uncle Tom's Cabin*, Clarke, Beeton, and Co. London, 1853, p 141.

17 Mayer, Henry, *All on Fire, William Lloyd Garrison and the Abolition of Slavery*, W.W. Norton & Company, New York, London, 1998, p 500.

18 *The Daily Dispatch*, (Richmond, Va), December 06, 1859.

19 *The New "Reign of Terror" in the Slaveholding States*, edited by William Lloyd Garrison, Arno Press & New York Times, New York, 1969

20 *New York Tribune*, quoted in *The New "Reign of Terror" in the Slaveholding States*, p iii.

21 *New York Independent*, quoted in *The New "Reign of Terror" in the Slaveholding States*, p 42.

22 *New York Independent*, quoted in *The New "Reign of Terror" in the Slaveholding States*, pp 63, 64.

23 *Advertiser* (Ill), quoted in *The New "Reign of Terror" in the Slaveholding States*, p 110.

24 Schaller, Frederic, quoted in *The New "Reign of Terror" in the Slaveholding States*, pp 56-58.

25 *The Belfast (Me.) Age*, quoted in *The New "Reign of Terror" in the Slaveholding States*, pp 84,85.

26 *The New "Reign of Terror" in the Slaveholding States*, p 32.

27 *The New "Reign of Terror" in the Slaveholding States*, p 96.
28 *Norristown Herald*, quoted in *The New "Reign of Terror" in the Slaveholding States*, p 106.
29 A form of the word, "chivalry," was used twelve additional times in the pamphlet to emphasize the connection between Southern chivalry and the depraved, wicked conduct Northerners experienced in the South.

CHAPTER SIX

1 Waddy Thompson, Representative from South Carolina, quoted in Miller, William Lee, *Arguing About Slavery*, Alfred A. Knopf, New York, 1996, p 244.
2 Personal Narrative of Mr. Nehemiah Caulkins, In *American Slavery as it is: Testimony of a Thousand Witnesses*, Assembled by Reverend Theodore Dwight Weld and Angelina and Sarah Grimke, New York, American Anti-Slavery Society, 1839, (available at docsouth.unc.edu), p 16.
3 Personal Narrative of Mr. George A. Avery, Weld, p 173.
4 Personal Narrative of Sarah M. Grimke, Weld, p 22.

5   Personal Narrative of Reverend William Scales, Weld, p 68.

6   Personal Narrative of Reverend C. Stewart Renshaw, Weld, p 71.

7   Personal Narrative of Col Thatcher as told by George Kimball, Esq., Weld, p 172.

8   Personal Narrative of Sarah M. Grimke, Weld, p 24.

9   Personal Narrative of Reverend John O. Choules, Weld, p 39.

10 Stowe, Harriet Beecher, *The Key to Uncle Tom's Cabin*, Clarke, Beeton, and Co., London, 1853, available at etext. lib.virginia.edu, p 58.

11 General William H. Harrison in letter to General Simon Bolivar, Weld, p 117.

12 Personal Narrative of Mrs. Childs, Weld, p 124.

13 Personal Narrative of Mr William Ladd, Esq, Weld, p 86.

14 Jefferson, Thomas, *Notes on the State of Virginia*, edited by Willaim Peden, The University of North Carolina Press, Chapel Hill, 1955, p 162.

15 Thomas Jefferson to John Holmes, (discussing slavery and the Missouri question), Monticello, 22 April 1820.

CHAPTER SEVEN

1   Takaki, Ronald T., *A Pro-slavery Crusade, The Agitation to Reopen the*

African Slave Trade, New York, New York, 1971, p 2, 3.

2 Takaki, p 135-137.

3 Gourdin, Theo. S., Editor of the *Southern Confederacy*, Jacksonville, Fla, reprinted in Anderson Court House, (S.C.) *The Anderson intelligencer*, March 14, 1861.

4 Dew, Charles B., *Apostles of Disunion, Southern Secession Commissioners and the Causes of the Civil War*, (Charlottesville and London, 2001).

5 Camden (SC) *The Camden journal*, August 22, 1849.

6 Charlotte (N.C.) *The Western Democrat*, June 16, 1857.

7 Wendell Phillips, quoted in Henry Mayer, *All on Fire, William Lloyd Garrison and the Abolition of Slavery*, (New York and London, 1998), 629.

8 McKivigan, John R. *The War against Proslavery Religion, Abolitionism and the Northern Churches, 1830-1865*, (Ithaca and London, 1984), p 91.

9 Sloane, J. R. W. Reverend, preached in the Third reformed Presbyterian Church response to a sermon by Reverend Henry J. Van Dyke, Cadiz, Ohio *The Cadiz Democratic sentinel*, March 6, 1861,.

10 Resolutions of the Ohio Baptist State convention, Warren, Ohio, *Western Reserve chronicle*, November 26, 1862.

11 Warren, Ohio, *Western Reserve chronicle*, November 4, 1863.

12 *Memphis daily appeal.*, Memphis, Tenn., November 27, 1863.

13 *Memphis daily appeal*, Memphis, Tenn., May 7, 1863.

14 *Memphis daily appeal*, Memphis, Tenn., September 3, 1862.

15 James D. Richardson ed., *The Messages and Papers of Jefferson Davis and the Confederacy*, (New York, 1966), 103.

16 Richardson, p 218.

17 Richardson, pp 412, 413.

18 Richardson, p 567.

19 *Charleston Courier*, quoted in *Edgefield advertiser.*, Edgefield, South Carolina, February 4, 1863.

20 Swaney, Charles Baumer, *Episcopal Methodism and Slavery*, Negro Universities Press, New York, 1969, p 312.

21 Swaney, pp 312, 313.

22 *Semi-weekly Standard*, Raleigh, N.C. May 31, 1862.

23 *The Abingdon Virginian*, Abingdon, Va., November 14, 1862.

24 *Southern Baptist Convention, Edgefield advertiser.,* Edgefield S.C., May 20, 1863.

25 *Memphis Daily Appeal,* Memphis, Tenn., July 31, 1861.

26 Reverend Dr. Palmer, "A Vindication of Secession and the South," *Southern Presbyterian Review,* quoted in *Keowee courier,* Pickens Court House, S.C., June 22, 1861.

27 *Staunton spectator,* Staunton, Va., September 24, 1861.

28 Speech given by Reverend Dr. Palmer, quoted in *Edgefield advertiser.,* Edgefield, S.C., May 11, 1864.

29 *New Orleans daily crescent,* New Orleans, La., February 4, 1861.

30 *Weekly standard,* Raleigh, N.C., May 14, 1862.

31 *Semi-weekly standard,* Raleigh, N.C., October 24, 1862.

32 *Memphis Daily Appeal,* Memphis, Tenn., May 07, 1864.

33 Excerpt from Dr. Palmer's sermon to the Crescent Rifles, May 26, 1861. *New Orleans daily crescent,* New Orleans, La., May 27, 1861.

34 Reverend Grundy fast-day sermon, *Memphis Daily Appeal,* Memphis, Tennessee, June 23, 1861.

35 Sermon by Reverend Wilson, T.B. D.D., *Dallas Herald*, Dallas, Tex., June 12, 1861.

36 Wilson, *Dallas Herald*.

37 Wilson, *Dallas Herald*.

38 Jones, J. Wm., D.D., *Christ in the Camp; or Religion in Lee's Army*. B. F. Johnson & Co. Richmond, Va., 1887, p 14.

39 From a speech from Reverend Robert Ryland, D.D. quoted in Jones, pp 165, 166.

40 Jones, pp 231-233.

41 Jones, pp 231-233.

42 Jones, pp 235-237.

43 Jones, p 239.

44 Jones, p 239,240.

45 Richard Baxter to Sallie Bird, 22 May 1861, Quoted in *The Granite Farm Letters, Civil War Correspondence of Edgeworth & Sallie Bird*, Edited by John Rozier, The University of Georgia Press Athens and London, 1988, p 3.

46 Bird, p 167.

47 Bird, p 196.

48 Bird, p 202.

49 Bird, p 204.

50 Bird, p 219.

51 Belle Edmondson diary, March 27th, 1863, quoted in *A Lost Heroine of the Confederacy, The Diaries and Letters of*

Belle Edmondson, Edited by Loretta and William Galbraith, University Press of Mississippi, Jackson and London, 1990, p 17.

52 Edmondson, p 19.

53 Edmondson, p 81.

54 Edmondson, p 87.

55 Edmondson, p 126.

56 Edmondson, p 130.

57 Chesnut, Mary Boykin, *A Diary from Dixie*, edited by Ben Ames Williams, Houghton Mifflin Company, Boston, Ma, 1949, p 38.

58 Chesnut, p 334.

59 Chesnut, p 492.

60 Obituary for Edwin R. Sloan, *The western Democrat*, Charlotte, N. C., August 16, 1864.

61 Obituary for Capt. Joseph Adrian Williams, *Semi-weekly standard*, Raleigh, N. C., January 08, 1864.

62 Obituary for W. B. Hagens, *Edgefield advertiser*, Edgefield, S. C., April 29, 1863.

63 Bennett, William W., *A Narrative of the Great Revival which Prevailed in the Southern Armies*, Claxton, Remsen & Haffelfinger, Philadelphia, 1877, pp 60, 61, 112, 122, 127, 133-136, 141, 146-150, 152, 153, 161-171, 179,

180, 182, 183, 192, 193, 201-203, 248, 256, 257, 300, 301, 317, 318, 328, 329, 335, 336, 349, 350, 354, 355, 383, 388, 395-397, 402-404, 411, 412, 417, 418.

64 Bennett, p 164.

65 Bennett, p 318.

66 Bennett, p 162.

67 Bennett, pp 162,163.

68 Bennett, p 169.

69 Bennett, p 112.

70 Jones, p 205.

CHAPTER EIGHT

1 Blomquist, Ann K. and Robert A. Taylor, eds., *This Cruel War, The Civil War Letters of Grant and Malinda Taylor, 1862-1865*, Mercer University Press, Macon, Ga, 2000, pp 322-333.

2 A correspondent from North Carolina, quoted in the *Staunton Spectator.*, Staunton, Va., May 21, 1861.

3 McPherson, James M., *For Cause & Comrades, Why Men Fought in the Civil War*, Oxford University Press, New York, 1997, pp 20, 21.

4 Obituary of Whitfield Butler Brooks, *Edgefield advertiser*, Edgefield, S.C. June 29, 1864.

5 Obituary of E. O. Chambers, *Memphis daily appeal*, Memphis, Tenn. May

27, 1862. See also obituaries of Col. J. C. Simkius in *Edgefield Advertiser*, Edgefield, S.C., March 23, 1864, quoted from *Columbia Guardian*, Whitfield Butler Brooks in *Edgefield Advertiser*, Edgefield, S.C. June 29, 1864, B. D. F. King in *Memphis daily appeal*, Memphis, Tenn. November 19, 1862, Major A. Kyle Blevins in *Memphis Daily Appeal*, Memphis, Tenn., June 6, 1864, et cetera et cetera

6   Address of Congress of the Confederate States, printed in the *Staunton spectator*, Staunton, Va., March 1, 1864.

7   Richardson, pp 227, 228.

8   Address of Congress of the Confederate States, printed in the *Staunton Spectator*, Staunton, Va., March 01, 1864.

9   Lincoln, Abraham, Address at a Sanitary Fair, available at http://teachingamericanhistory. org/library/document/address-at-a-sanitary-fair/ accessed 12/17/2015.

10 Address of Congress of the Confederate states, printed in the *Staunton spectator*, Staunton, Va., March 01, 1864.

11 *Winchester Daily Bulletin*, Winchester, Tenn., May 22, 1863.

12 Parson W. G. Brownlow, *Memphis Daily Appeal*, Memphis, Tenn., September 29, 1862.

13 Stephen Elliott, "Ezra's Dilemma," August 21, 1863, in David B.

Chesebrough, ed., *"God Ordained This War" Sermons on the Sectional Crisis, 1830-1865*, University of South Carolina Press, Columbia, South Carolina, 1991, p. 248.

14 Swaney, Charles Baumer, *Episcopal Methodism and Slavery*, Negro Universities Press, New York, 1969, p. 321.

15 Swaney, p 332.

16 Reverend T.B. Wilson, D.D. in a sermon to his congregation in Marshall, Texas, *Dallas Herald*, June 12, 1861.

17 Smith, George G., *The Life and Times of George Foster Pierce, D.D., LL. D., Bishop of the Episcopal Church, South* (Sparta, Ga., 1888), 488.

18 Stowell, Daniel W., *Rebuilding Zion, The Religious Reconstruction of the South*, 1863-1877, Oxford University Press, New York, New York, 1998, p 32.

19 Burr, Virginia Ingraham, ed. *The Secret Eye: The Journal of Ella Gertrude Clanton Thomas*, 1848-1889. Chapel Hill: The University of North Carolina Press, 1990, p 277. October 8, 1865. Quoted in Culpepper, Marilyn Mayer, *Women of the Civil War South*, McFarland & Company, Inc, 2004, pp 229-230.

20 Wilson, Charles Reagan, *Baptized in Blood, The Religion of the Lost Cause,*

1865-1930, The University of Georgia Press, Athens, Ga., 1980, pp 21, 22.

21 Hoge, Peyton Harrison, *Moses Drury Hoge: Life and Letters*, Presbyterian Committee of Publication, Richmond, Va., 1899, p 230.

22 Hoge, p 230.

23 Hoge, p 230.

24 Hoge, p 235.

25 Brandon, Zillah. *Diaries* (SPR 262). Alabama Department of Archives and History. Montgomery, Alabama. July 6, 1965, Quoted in Culpepper, Marilyn Mayer, *Women of the Civil War South*, McFarland & Company, Inc, 2004, p 232.

26 Governor McDuffie's "Message on the Slavery Question," 1835, pp. 4-5, quoted in "*The Debate over Slavery*," David F. Ericson, New York University Press, 2000, p 19.

27 Prayer of Reverend J. William Jones, quoted in Wilson, Charles Reagan, *Baptized in Blood, The Religion of the Lost Cause, 1865-1920*, The University of Georgia Press, Athens, Ga., 1980, p 133.

28 Reverend J. Wm. Jones, DD, Christ in the Camp; or Religion in Lee's Army. B. F. Johnson & Co. Richmond, Va., 1887, pp 245, 246.

29 Jones, p 260.

30 Jones, p 261.

31 Bennett, William W., *A Narrative of the Great Revival which Prevailed in the Southern Armies*, Claxton, Remsen & Haffelfinger, Philadelphia, 1877, pp 364, 365.

32 Pollard, Edward A., *The Lost Cause, A New Southern History of the War of the Confederates*, E. B. Treate & Co., New York, 1866, p 3.

33 Pollard, Edward A., "*The Lost Cause, A New Southern History of the War of the Confederates*," E. B. Treat & Co., Publishers, New York, 1866, p 47.

34 Pollard, p 49.

35 Arthur M. Schlesinger, Jr. "A Note on Historical Sentimentalism," as quoted in Rozwenc, p 187.

36 Orrin S. Ferry, Republican Congressman from Connecticut on Committee of Thirty-three dealing with secessionist crisis, quoted in *Slavery as a Cause of the Civil War*, edited by Edwin C. Rozwenc, D. C. Heath and Company, Boston, 1963, pp 35, 36.

37 Sarah Grimke, quoted in Miller, William Lee, *Arguing about Slavery*, Alfred A. Knopf, New York, 1996, p. 495.

38 Douglass, Frederick, "What To the Slave Is the Fourth of July," quoted in the Oxford Frederick Douglass Reader, Ed. William L. Andrews, New York: Oxford UP, 1996, pp. 123, 124.

39 Mayer, , Henry, *All on Fire, William Lloyd Garrison and the Abolition of Slavery*, W. W. Norton & Company, New York, London, 1998, p 65.

40 Mayer, p 475.

41 Stowe, Harriet Beecher, *Uncle Tom's Cabin*, Pocket Books, New York, London, Toronto, Sydney, chapter 29.

42 James Ford Rhodes, Slavery as a Single Cause, as quoted in *The Causes of the American Civil War*, Edited by Edwin C. Rozwenc, D. C. Heath and Company, 1961, p 86.

43 Eugene D. Genovese and Elizabeth Fox-Genovese, in *Looking South, Chapters in the Story of an American Region*, Edited by Winfred B. Moore, Jr. and Joseph R. Tripp, Greenwood Press, New York, Westport Connecticut, London, 1989, p 39.

CHAPTER NINE

1 Wilson, Charles Reagan, *Baptized in Blood, The Religion of the Lost Cause, 1865-1920*, (Athens, Ga., 2009), pp 6, 11, 37, 58.

2 *The Myth of the Lost Cause and Civil War History*, edited by Gary W. Gallagher and Alan T. Nolan, Indiana University Press, Bloomington and Indianapolis, 2000, p 1.

3 Captain Robert E. Lee, Son of General Robert E. Lee, *Recollections and Letters of General Robert E. Lee*, Doubleday, Page & Company, 1905, pp 105, 106.

4 http://www.indiana.edu/~liblilly/history/generaltext.html, accessed 2/25/2016.

5 *The Myth of the Lost Cause and Civil War History*, edited by Gary W. Gallagher and Alan T. Nolan, Indiana University Press, Bloomington and Indianapolis, 2000, p 96.

6 Calhoun's Speech on the Compromise of 1850, From *Congressional Globe*, 31sst Congress, 1st Session. Volume 22, part 1 (1850). 451-455.

7 Richard Baxter to Sallie Bird, 22 May 1861, Quoted in *The Granite Farm Letters, Civil War Correspondence of Edgeworth & Sallie Bird*, edited by John Rozier, The University of Georgia Press, Athens and London, 1988, p 145.

8 Sean Wilentz, "The Lost Cause and the Won Case," New Republic, 243, Issue 20, (12/31/2012); William J. Cooper Jr. "The Critical Signpost on

the Journey Toward Secession," The
Journal of Southern History, LXXVII,
No. 1, (February 2011).

9 Pew Research Center website. www.
pewresearch.org/question-search/?key
word=cause+of+the+civil+war, April 8,
2011, accessed 2/25/2016.

10 Dew, Charles B., *Apostles of Disunion,
Southern Secession Commissioners and
the Causes of the Civil War*, University
Press of Virginia, Charlottesville and
London, 2001, p. 2.

11 William L. Harris address, quoted in
Dew, pp 85, 89.

12 Letter from Stephen F. Hale to the
governor of Kentucky, quoted in Dew,
p 98.

13 Dew, pp 76-81.

14 http://teachingamericanhistory.org/
library/document/farewell-speech/,
accessed 12/18/2015.

15 Thomas Jefferson, *Notes on the state of
Virginia*, ed. William Peden. Chapel
Hill, N.C: University of North
Caroline Press, 1955, p 163.

16 Scott, Walter, *Ivanhoe*, American Book
Company, New York, 1892, p 54.

17 DeRosa Marshall L., *Confederate
Constitution of 1861, An Inquiry into
American Constitutionalism*, University
of Missouri Press, Columbia, Mo,
1991, p 148.

18 DeRosa, p 149.

19 Dew, pp 4, 16.

20 Dew, p 75.

21 Gallagher, *Myth of the Lost Cause,* p 96.

22 *Charleston Courier,* November 1, 1860, quoted in Lorman A. Ratner and Dwight L. Teeter Jr., *"Fanatics and Fire-eaters, Newspapers and the Coming of the Civil War,"* University of Illinois Press, Urbana and Chicago, 2003, p 93.

23 Spratt, L. W., Philosophy of Secession: A Southern View; Letter addressed to Mr. Perkins, February 13, 1861, http://docsouth.unc.edu/imls/secession/secession.html, accessed 2/25/2016

24 Republican Party Platforms: "Republican Party Platform of 1860," May 17, 1860. Online by Gerhard Peters and John T. Woolley, The American Presidency Project. http://www.presidency.ucsb.edu/ws/?pid=29620, accessed 2/25/2016.

25 Northup, Solomon, *Twelve Years a Slave,* Derby and Miller, Auburn, 1853, pp 259, 260.

26 Northup, p 121.

27 Northup, p 121.

28 Chesnut, Mary Boykin, *A Diary from Dixie,* Edited by Ben Ames Williams,

Houghton Mifflin Company, Boston, Ma, 1949, pp 21, 22.

29 Chesnut. P 418.

30 Chesnut, p 468.

31 Chesnut, p 140.

32 Chesnut, p 147.

33 Chesnut, p 158.

34 Pollard, pp 41, 42.

35 http://www.constitution.org/ jm/18300828_everett.txt, accessed 12/18/2015.

36 Lincoln, Abraham, Message to Congress in Special Session, July 4, 1861, quoted in Roxwenc, p 45.

37 Gallagher, p 111.

38 Gallagher, pp 196, 197.

39 Cobb, James C., "How Did Robert E. Lee Become an American Icon?" *Humanities*, Jul/Aug 2001, vol. 32, Issue 4, 28-33.

40 Gallagher, pp 199, 200.

41 Watson, Harry L., *Liberty and Power, The Politics of Jacksonian America*, Hill and Wang, New York, 1990, p 166.

42 Pollard, p 47, 49.

43 Miller, William Lee, *Arguing about Slavery*, Alfred A. Knopf, New York, 1996, p 371.

44 Gallagher, p 1.

45 Obituary of Major Jas. S. Whitehead, Raleigh (N.C.) *Semi-Weekly Standard*, August 20, 1862.

46 Obituary of Lieutenant Thomas Riddick, Raleigh (N.C.) *Weekly Standard*, December 3, 1862. See also Griffin (Ga.) *The daily Chattanooga rebel*, July 25, 1864; Raleigh (N.C.) *Weekly Standard*, November 12, 1862; Raleigh (N.C.) *Weekly Standard*, February 4, 1863; Raleigh (N.C.) *Weekly Standard*, August 6, 1862; and Raleigh (N.C.) *Weekly Standard*, August 13, 1862.

47 Stowell, Daniel W., *Rebuilding Zion, The Religious Reconstruction of the South, 1863-1877*, Oxford University Press, New York, New York, 1998, p 180.

48 Dunham, Chester Forrester, *The Attitude of the Northern Clergy Toward the South 1860-1865* (Philadelphia, 1974), 194-196.

49 Dunham, 204-237.

50 Wilson, 65-70.

51 Rozwenc, p v.

52 http://encyclopediavirginia.org/lost_cause_the#its1, accessed 2/25/2016.

CHAPTER TEN

1 Wills, pp 334-351.

2 Mayer, Henry, *All on Fire, William Lloyd Garrison and the Abolition of*

Slavery, W. W. Norton & Company, New York, London, 1998, p 51.

3 Mayer, p 38.

4 Mayer, pp 44, 45.

5 Mayer, pp 51, 78, 427.

6 Mayer, pp 53, 139, 233-236, 629.

7 Mayer, pp 102,103.

8 Mayer, p 229.

9 Swaney, Charles Baumer, *Episcopal Methodism and Slavery*, Negro Universities Press, New York, 1969, p 51.

10 Mayer, p 65.

11 Douglass, Frederick, "What To the Slave Is the Fourth of July," quoted in the *Oxford Frederick Douglass Reader*, Ed. William L. Andrews, New York: Oxford UP, 1996, pp 124, 125.

12 Mayer, pp 175, 213-215.

13 Mayer, p 78.

14 Mayer, p 519.

15 Mayer, p 593.

16 Swaney, p 323.

17 Ritner, Jacob to Emeline Ritner, May 16, 1861, quoted in Love and Valor, Charles F. Larimer, ed. *Intimate Civil War Letters Between Captain Jacob and Emeline Ritner*, (Western Springs, Il, Sigourney Press, Inc., 2000), 22.

18 Mayer, pp 520-547.

19 Swaney, p 329.

20 Don E. Fehrenbacher and Virginia Fehrenbacher, *Recollected Words of Abraham Lincoln*, Stanford University Press, Stanford, Calif., 1996, p 474, quoted in Noll, Mark A., *The Civil War as a Theological Crisis*, The University of North Carolina Press, Chapel Hill, N.C., 2006, p 89.

21 Davis, William C., *The Cause Lost, Myths and Realities of the Confederacy*, University Press of Kansas, 1996, p 114.

22 Davis, p 121.

23 *The Daily Dispatch*, Richmond Va., July 4, 1863.

24 Elliott, "Ezra's Dilemma," In Cheesebrough, *"God ordained this War:" sermons of the sectional crisis, 1830-1865"* p 247.

25 Swaney, p 332.

26 Swaney, p 321.

27 Oates, William C., *The War Between the Union and the Confederacy and Its Lost Opportunities*, The Neale Publishing Company, New York and Washington, 1905, p 247.

CHAPTER ELEVEN

1 Speech given by Carl Schurz at Springfield, Mass., quoted in *Daily*

Dispatch, Richmond, Va., April 10, 1861, available at chroniclingamerica. loc.gov.

2 http://www.birtherreport. com/2014/11/full-video-presentation-of.html, accessed December 2, 2015.

3 http://www.birtherreport. com/2014/11/failed-e-verify-letter-to-obama.html, accessed December 2, 2015.

CHAPTER TWELVE

1 http://www.hebcal.com/converter, accessed July 8, 2015.

2 Biltz, Mark, *Blood Moons, Decoding the Imminent Heavenly Signs*, WND Books, 2014, pp 143-156.

3 Bullinger, E.W., *Number in Scripture*, Kregel Publications, Grand Rapids, MI, p 235.